The St. Paul Way, Truth and Life Series

HIS SAVING LOVE

Written by a Team of Daughters of St. Paul

Based on the most recent catechetical documents

This book belongs to _____

St. Paul Catechetical Center

NIHIL OBSTAT:
Rev. Thomas W. Buckley, S.T.D., S.S.L.
Censor Deputatus

IMPRIMATUR:
✞ Humberto Cardinal Medeiros
Archbishop of Boston

Copyright © 1982, 1980, by the Daughters of St. Paul

Printed in the U.S.A. by the Daughters of St. Paul
50 St. Paul's Ave., Boston, MA 02130

The Daughters of St. Paul are an international congregation of religious women serving the Church with the communications media.

Excerpts from the **New American Bible** [indicated by one asterisk (*)], copyright © 1970, by the Confraternity of Christian Doctrine, Washington, D.C., are used by permission of copyright owner. All rights reserved.

Excerpts from **The Jerusalem Bible**, [indicated by two asterisks (**)] copyright © 1966 by Darton, Longman & Todd, Ltd. and Doubleday and Company, Inc. Used by permission of the publisher.

ISBN 0-8198-0340-5

HIS SAVING LOVE is the seventh grade text of the ST. PAUL RELIGION SERIES, which includes the St. Paul WAY, TRUTH AND LIFE elementary series and the DIVINE MASTER high school series.

The St. Paul Religion Series was produced by a team of Daughters of St. Paul of the American Province under the direction of Very Rev. James Alberione, S.S.P., S.T.D. The Sisters hold degrees in catechetics, theology, education, philosophy, communications, and art.

THE TEAM OF AUTHORS:

Sister Concetta Beleggia
Sister Mary Catherine Devine
Sister Mary Anne Heffernan
Sister Mary Helen Wallace

EDITORIAL ASSISTANTS: Sr. Davina Louise Edwards, Sr. M. Vincent MacNamara, Sr. M. Gemma Stewart, Sr. M. Clement Turcotte, Sr. M. Mark Wickenhiser.

ART AND LAYOUT: Sr. M. Charles Dangrow, Sr. Mary Alphonse Martineau, Sr. Marie Immaculate Morrison, Sr. M. Bernardine Sattler.

CREDITS:

DSP Studio
G. DeLuca

Chiarella: 56, 69 top
Crocella: 68 bottom, 69 bottom, 100-101
Dolan: 4 bottom
Ghilardi: 110
St. Gabriel High School, New Rochelle: 11 top

Daughters of St. Paul

IN MASSACHUSETTS
  50 St. Paul's Ave., Jamaica Plain, Boston, MA 02130;
  617-522-8911; 617-522-0875
  172 Tremont Street, Boston, MA 02111; **617-426-5464;**
  617-426-4230
IN NEW YORK
  78 Fort Place, Staten Island, NY 10301; **212-447-5071**
  59 East 43rd Street, New York, NY 10017; **212-986-7580**
  625 East 187th Street, Bronx, NY 10458; **212-584-0440**
  525 Main Street, Buffalo, NY 14203; **716-847-6044**
IN NEW JERSEY
  Hudson Mall — Route 440 and Communipaw Ave.,
  Jersey City, NJ 07304; **201-433-7740**
IN CONNECTICUT
  202 Fairfield Ave., Bridgeport, CT 06604; **203-335-9913**
IN OHIO
  2105 Ontario St. (at Prospect Ave.), Cleveland, OH 44115; **216-621-9**
  25 E. Eighth Street, Cincinnati, OH 45202; **513-721-4838**
IN PENNSYLVANIA
  1719 Chestnut Street, Philadelphia, PA 19103; **215-568-2638**
IN VIRGINIA
  1025 King St., Alexandria, VA 22314 **703-683-1741**
IN FLORIDA
  2700 Biscayne Blvd., Miami, FL 33137; **305-573-1618**
IN LOUISIANA
  4403 Veterans Memorial Blvd., Metairie, LA 70002; **504-887-7631;**
  504-887-0113
  1800 South Acadian Thruway, P.O. Box 2028, Baton Rouge, LA 70821
  504-343-4057; 504-343-3814

IN MISSOURI
  1001 Pine Street (at North 10th), St. Louis, MO 63101; **314-621-0346;**
  314-231-1034
IN ILLINOIS
  172 North Michigan Ave., Chicago, IL 60601; **312-346-4228**
  312-346-3240
IN TEXAS
  114 Main Plaza, San Antonio, TX 78205; **512-224-8101**
IN CALIFORNIA
  1570 Fifth Avenue, San Diego, CA 92101; **714-232-1442**
  46 Geary Street, San Francisco, CA 94108; **415-781-5180**
IN HAWAII
  1143 Bishop Street, Honolulu, HI 96813; **808-521-2731**
IN ALASKA
  750 West 5th Avenue, Anchorage AK 99501; **907-272-8183**
IN CANADA
  3022 Dufferin Street, Toronto 395, Ontario, Canada
IN ENGLAND
  128, Notting Hill Gate, London W11 3QG, England
  133 Corporation Street, Birmingham B4 6PH, England
  5A-7 Royal Exchange Square, Glasgow G1 3AH, England
  82 Bold Street, Liverpool L1 4HR, England
IN AUSTRALIA
  58 Abbotsford Rd., Homebush, N.S.W., Sydney 2140, Australia

CONTENTS

1. A Book That Lives and Speaks 4

Salvation's Story Begins
UNIT ONE
2. Our Need To Be Saved 8
3. The First Great Believer 12
4. Rescue! 16
5. The Flaming Mountain 21
6. Priestly People 26

Toward the Fullness of Time
UNIT TWO
7. Land of the Promise 30
8. Three Men and a Kingdom 36
9. A Nation Crumbles 40
10. New Challenges, New Heroes 45
11. Other Biblical "Whats" and "Whys" 50

He Comes To Live Among Us
UNIT THREE
12. The Mystery of Jesus 55
13. Echoes of the Exodus 60
14. Bread for God's People 64
15. His Closest Followers 69
16. Man for Others 75

Light Battles Darkness
UNIT FOUR
17. He Spoke Up for Jesus 80
18. Life Restored—Death Decreed 85
19. No Limits to Love 90
20. A Glimpse of Worlds Beyond 95
21. The Mysterious Victory 100

His Saving Mission Continues
UNIT FIVE
22. Sunrise! 106
23. Courage from the Spirit 111
24. The Thirteenth Apostle 116
25. A Great Runner—A Great Race 121
26. To the Ends of the Earth 128

Prayers .... inside front and back covers
Guidelines for Christian Living 133
Some Basic Truths of our Faith 134
Listing of Biblical Pictures 136
Glossary 137
Index 143

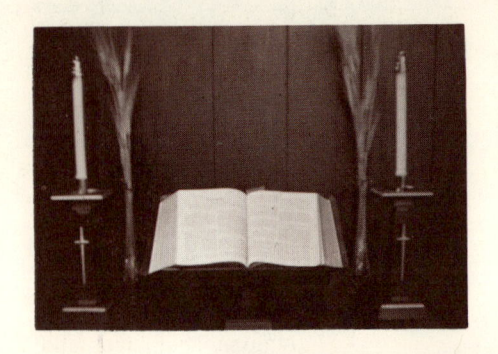

1 A BOOK THAT LIVES AND SPEAKS

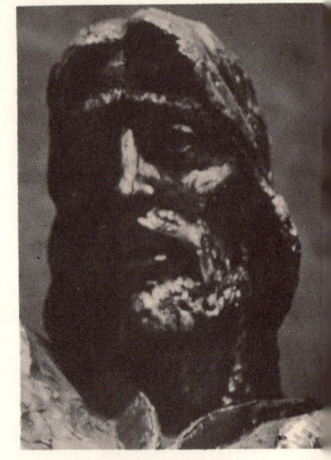

The apostles couldn't believe their eyes. True, two of Jesus' disciples had just arrived, breathless, from Emmaus with the astounding news that their Leader truly **had** risen from the dead. But now that Jesus Himself actually stood before them in the darkening room, they were completely speechless.

"Peace be with you," the risen Lord said quietly. But no one returned His greeting. Fear froze the apostles' hearts and tongues. Was it a ghost standing before them?

Gently the Master (Teacher) tried to calm them. He showed them the marks of the wounds in His wrists and feet, invited them to touch Him, and finally asked whether they had anything there to eat. Only when the apostles had watched Him consume a piece of grilled fish did they begin to accept the stupendous reality of the resurrection. And we can imagine their joy!

Then, St. Luke tells us, Jesus explained that His suffering, death and resurrection had been foretold in the Scriptures—in what we today would call the Old Testament of the Bible. He said:

"This is what I meant when I said, while I was still with you, that everything written about me in the Law of Moses, in the Prophets and in the Psalms, has to be fulfilled." He then opened their minds to understand the scriptures, and he said to them, "So you see how it is written that the Christ would suffer and on the third day rise from the dead, and that, in his name, repentance for the forgiveness of sins would be preached to all the nations, beginning from Jerusalem. You are witnesses to this."

(Luke 24:44-48)**

So even the Old Testament speaks about Jesus? Yes, for Jesus is the goal of all the history of the Old Testament. And He is the reason for the part of the Bible called the New Testament. In fact, the central fact of the whole Bible is Jesus Christ—the Son of God, who became man to teach us, to show us the way to heaven, to give His very life for us.

This is why the Bible is so important to Catholics and many other people. It tells us about God's great saving actions—how He has worked in and through history to free people from sin and bring them to Himself. And it tells us what we are to believe and do in order to **receive** the salvation that Jesus won for us with His death and resurrection.

So through the Bible (also called SCRIPTURE, or "the writings"), we learn about God and His plans for us. To help us in this learning process, we also have DIVINE TRADITION—teachings of Jesus that were not written down by the first Christians but were passed on from the apostles through their successors. Both the Bible and Tradition make up what is called REVELATION (G). They are explained to us by the CHURCH (G), which is guided by God the Holy Spirit and continues Jesus' saving work in our own times.

What is the Bible? The Word of God—our loving Father's letter to us. This "letter" was written down by men under God's INSPIRATION. Inspiration means special guidance given by the Holy Spirit in order that the Bible would contain only what God wanted written.

---

1. This word is explained in the glossary. Throughout the text, any word followed by (G) will be found in the glossary.

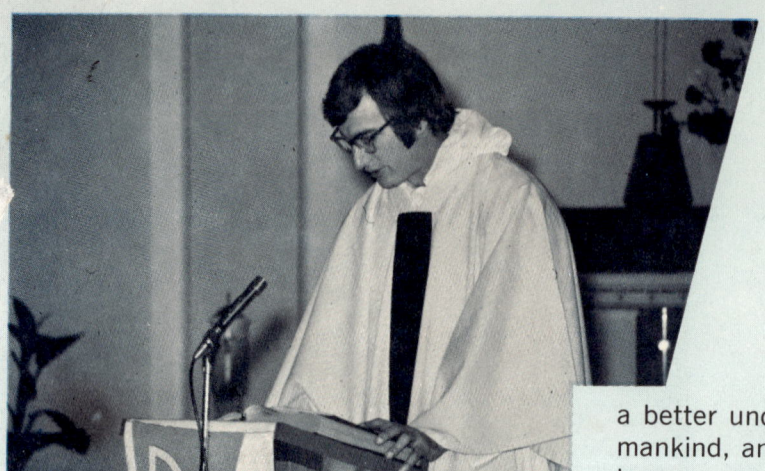

The word BIBLE means "book." The Bible is made up of 73 parts, and each of these is also called a book. Each book reflects the personality and style of its human author and the times in which he lived. And each was written for a particular purpose. There are histories, collections of laws for the chosen people, stories that teach, prayer songs, collections of wise sayings, letters to Christian communities, and so forth.

46 of these books make up the OLD TESTAMENT, written before the birth of Jesus. "Testament" here refers to the great covenant, or friendship agreement, made between God and the chosen people. With loving care called divine Providence, God guided His people step by step toward a better understanding of Him, of mankind, and of His plans for the human race.

The NEW TESTAMENT is composed of 27 books. It centers around Jesus, who became one of us and showed God's love for man in the clearest and most perfect way. By His teachings and example, by His life-giving death and resurrection, He made it possible for us to enter into the joy of the Blessed Trinity in heaven after our life on earth is ended. Jesus offered and still offers a new and everlasting covenant to all mankind. As His baptized followers, we are people of the new covenant—the new people of God.

When was the Bible written? Over a period of centuries. Often the contents of an Old Testament book would be passed on by word of mouth from one generation to another before they were collected and written down. Something similar happened with the Gospels, although not over such a long period.

Where was the Bible written? In many different places—the Old Testament in Palestine, Babylon, Egypt...and the New Testament in Palestine, Greece, Rome....

In what languages was it written? Chiefly in Hebrew and in Greek. Our English Bibles are translations. This explains why the English wording of

Catholic Bibles may vary, although the meaning remains the same.

What does the Bible mean for us today? Very much. Together with the Eucharist—which is the Body and Blood of Jesus Christ Himself—the Bible is meant to be the spiritual food of every Catholic Christian.

Reading the Bible, we discover God's loving, saving actions in history. This helps us to see them in our own lives, too, for the history of salvation has not yet ended. God is still drawing His people toward Himself.

Reading the Bible, we come to see what the "man of God" is like—how we should live in order to return God's great love for us.

Reading the Bible, we find the solutions to problems that come up in our lives.

Reading the Bible, we come to understand God and ourselves better.

Reading the Bible, we find beautiful prayers with which to adore God, thank Him, ask His forgiveness or ask His help.

Can you think of other reasons for reading the Bible?

Suggested Readings: Luke 24:36-48; John 20:19-21

What is the Bible's main theme?

The Bible's main theme is God's love for man, which was especially shown by Jesus Christ in His life, teachings, death and resurrection.

What are the main parts of the Bible?

The Bible is made up of the Old Testament, which contains 46 parts called books, and the New Testament, which contains 27 books.

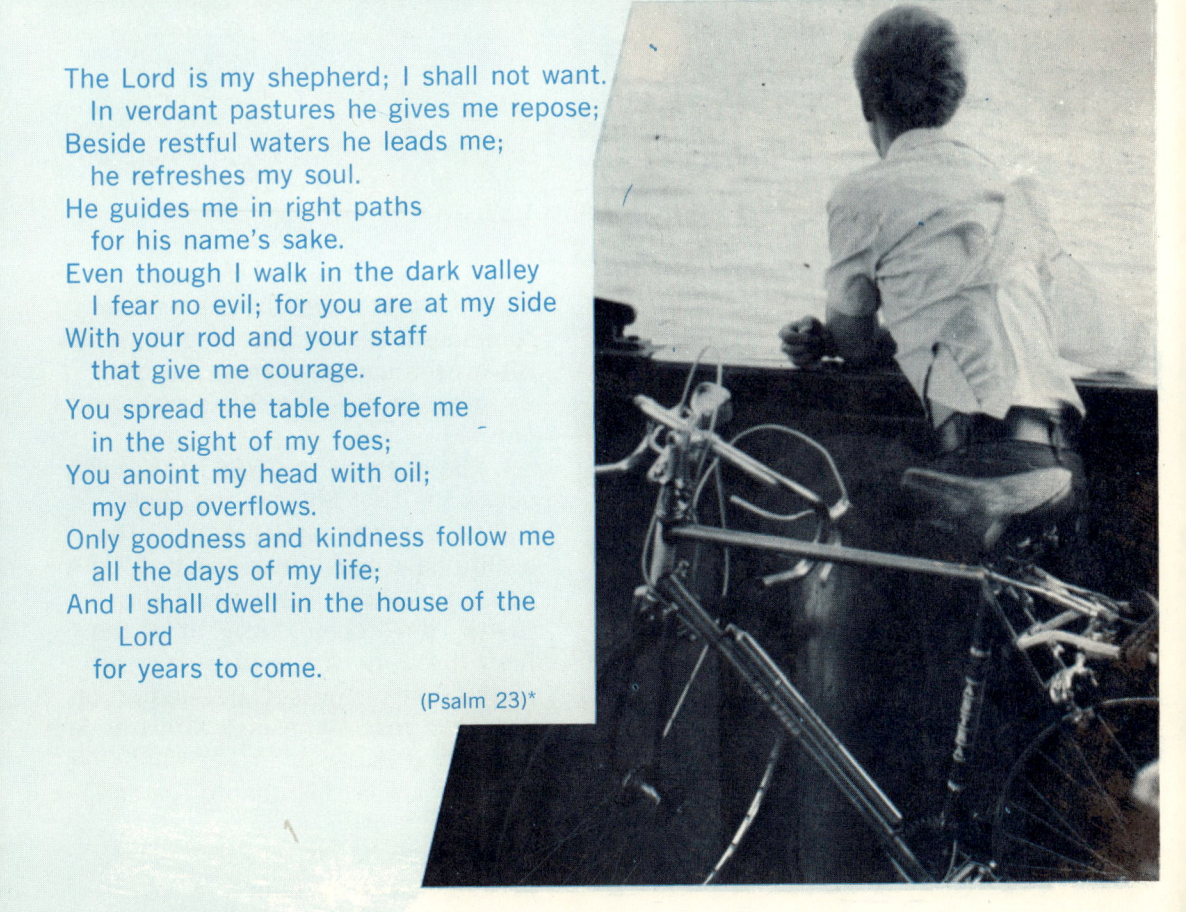

The Lord is my shepherd; I shall not want.
   In verdant pastures he gives me repose;
Beside restful waters he leads me;
   he refreshes my soul.
He guides me in right paths
   for his name's sake.
Even though I walk in the dark valley
   I fear no evil; for you are at my side
With your rod and your staff
   that give me courage.
You spread the table before me
   in the sight of my foes;
You anoint my head with oil;
   my cup overflows.
Only goodness and kindness follow me
   all the days of my life;
And I shall dwell in the house of the Lord
   for years to come.
              (Psalm 23)*

Unit 1 Salvation's Story Begins

2 OUR NEED TO BE SAVED

In the Book of Isaiah (chapter 40), God asks His people:

Who has cupped in his hand the waters of the sea,
  and marked off the heavens with a span?
Who has held in a measure the dust of the earth,
  weighed the mountains in scales and the hills in a balance?
Who has directed the spirit of the Lord,
  or has instructed him as his counselor?...
Behold, the nations count as a drop of the bucket,
  as dust on the scales....
                    (Isaiah 40:12-13, 15)*

In a poetic type of expression common in the ancient Near East, the Bible uses concrete images (word pictures) to describe God's power over nature.

The account of CREATION which opens the first book of the Bible (called Genesis) is also poetic. The events have been arranged to form a pattern in which the work of the fourth "day" completes that of the first, the work of the fifth day completes that of the second, and so on. When we read Genesis 1 with this fact in mind, it is easier to see what God is telling us in this chapter of Scripture:

—There is only **one** God, who existed before the universe.

— All things are His creatures.
— The universe and everything in it were created for our **good.**
— God Himself is good, and He is wise.
— Man is higher than the plants and animals. He is made to God's "image and likeness"—meaning that he is able to **know** and to **make decisions** (powers which no other material creatures have).

In Genesis 2:5, a second account of creation begins. This one is given with many more word pictures. Again, it emphasizes man's superiority over the rest of God's visible creation. The images used in this account show us that men and women are equal in human dignity and that marriage is meant to last.

What about evolution? The Bible isn't a scientific textbook, so we can't expect to find evolution treated in the Book of Genesis. But there is no conflict between the Bible and science. If there **was** evolution, only God—with His marvelous intelligence—could have been responsible for it.

What we have just said regards evolution **in general.** But concerning our **first parents** we needn't worry, either. Every human being has a spiritual soul, created directly by God. The same would have been true of the first human beings. They became human beings when they received their souls from God. Therefore, we can truly say that He **created** our first parents.

What were their names? The Bible very appropriately calls them: Adam, which means **man** (and is related to the Hebrew word for clay), and Eve, which is related to the Hebrew word **living,** "because she was the mother of all the living" (Genesis 3:20).*

The images used in the second chapter of Genesis tell us that God showered His goodness on our first parents through many wonderful gifts, which included the closeness to Him that we now call grace (G). We learn more about these special gifts when we read the next chapter of Genesis, which tells us that these gifts were lost.

In Genesis 3 we find our first parents facing temptation and giving in to it. Again, we look beyond the word pictures of the story to see what meaning God wanted to convey to the chosen people and to us. The meaning is this:
— Man was created free from sin.
— Man rebelled against God in pride and disobedience.
— As a result, he became subject to the devil, to sickness and death, to error, to strong desires to commit sin. Worst of all, he was no longer God's close friend through grace.
— God did not abandon man to despair, but offered a mysterious promise of a battle between the woman's offspring and the devil, a battle which the devil would lose.

9

In this chapter of Genesis we find the first mention of angels that is made in the Bible. From revelation, as explained to us by the Church, we know that the angels are pure spirits (living beings that have nothing material about them). We also know that some of the angels turned away from God and became devils. It was the devil who tempted our first parents to sin. He also tempts **us.** In the First Epistle of Peter we read that the devil is "prowling like a roaring lion, looking for someone to devour" (1 Peter 5:8).*

It was because of our first parents' sin that the story of SALVATION began. Salvation means "saving," and we all need to be saved. Each of us comes into the world without grace, a condition called ORIGINAL SIN. And we all experience the same **effects** of original sin that our first parents experienced after their rebellion against God—the loss of His special gifts. No human being has a right to these gifts (complete self-control, great knowledge, freedom from sickness and death), so God was completely **just** (G) in taking them away from mankind.

But God is also **merciful** (G). He loves and forgives. Salvation history in the Old Testament, in the New Testament, and in the life of the Church is the story of God's saving actions in the lives of men. The center, or focal point, of salvation history is Jesus Christ, who became man, died and rose for our sake. Because of Jesus, we share in God's own life (grace) and have the opportunity of living with Him forever in heaven. St. Paul says:

For anyone who is in Christ, there is a new creation; the old creation has gone, and now the new one is here.

(2 Corinthians 5:17)**

There are many ways that we can apply to our own lives the truths taught in chapters 1-3 of Genesis.

For example, God gave us our intelligence, our willpower and even our hands so that we might cooperate with Him in keeping our world good, as He made it, and working for the peace, progress and happiness of our fellow men. We are God's "partners" in building up a better world.

We are also "priests of creation" —that is, we can praise and thank God in the name of all His lower creatures, who don't have the intelligence needed for this.

And we belong to the "new creation" by grace. Therefore, with God's help, we are to fight against sin and overcome it.

Can you think of other ways in which these chapters of the Bible apply to our own lives?

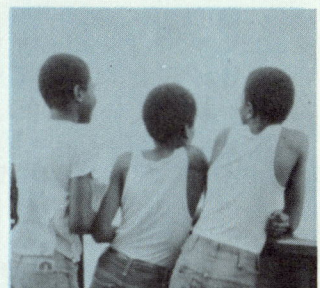

Suggested Readings: Genesis, chapters 1-3

What do we mean by salvation history?
By salvation history we mean that from the beginning of history God has been acting to save mankind—to free people from sin and help them to lead good lives in order that they may be happy in this life and in the next. The center of salvation history (and of **all** history) is Jesus Christ, our Savior.

Bless the Lord, O my soul!
  O Lord, my God, you are great indeed!
You are clothed with majesty and glory,
  robed in light as with a cloak.
You have spread out the heavens like a tent-cloth;
  you have constructed your palace upon the waters.
You make the clouds your chariot;
  you travel on the wings of the wind....
You fixed the earth upon its foundation,
  not to be moved forever....
You made the moon to mark the seasons;
  the sun knows the hour of its setting....
How manifold are your works, O Lord!
  In wisdom you have wrought them all—
    the earth is full of your creatures.
        (Psalm 104:1-3, 5, 19, 24)*

3 THE FIRST GREAT BELIEVER

The chief message of chapters 4-11 of Genesis is man's continuing sinfulness. This point is made in the stories of Cain and Abel, the flood, and the tower of Babel. In the account of Noah and the ark we can also see God's hatred for sin and His loving concern for all mankind.

Looking at these chapters of Genesis from a New-Testament viewpoint, we might also think of the ark and the waters as **typifying** —that is, foreshadowing—the Church (the "boat of Peter") and Baptism (see 1 Peter 3:20-22).

Genesis 12 puts us in touch with one of the great figures of salvation history. His name was Abram—later changed by God to ABRAHAM. He has been called "the friend of God," the father of the chosen people, and our own father in faith.

Abraham lived around the nineteenth century B.C. Together with his father, Terah, and the rest of their clan, he left his home city of Ur in lower Mesopotamia and journeyed to Haran, about five hundred miles to the northwest. There they lived as seminomads (G), raising great flocks and herds and acquiring many servants.

And then Abraham experienced God's call. To understand what a breakthrough this was, we have to consider the world in which Abraham lived. It was thoroughly pagan. Immorality (bad living—sin) was everywhere; in fact, it was greatly involved in pagan religions.

This was the type of world in which Abraham was called—perhaps through a vision, perhaps in some other way—to believe in and worship the one, true God. And, even more, he was told:

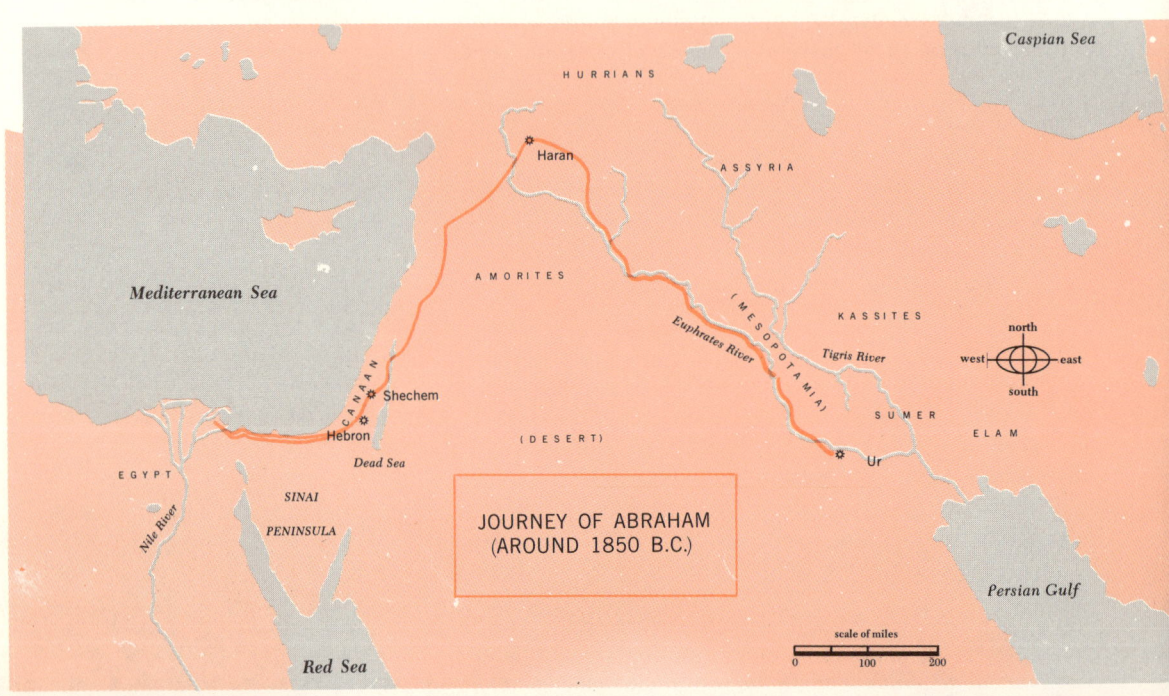

JOURNEY OF ABRAHAM (AROUND 1850 B.C.)

"Go forth from the land of
your kinsfolk and from your father's
house to a land that I will show you.
"I will make of you a great nation
and I will bless you....
All the communities of the earth
shall find blessing in you."

(Genesis 12:1-3)*

What a promise! A man who was childless and already growing old would become the ancestor of an entire nation! And because of him all the peoples of the earth would be blessed!

It wasn't easy to pull up stakes again at his age and leave behind all the members of his clan except his wife, Sarah, and his nephew, Lot. But Abraham put his trust in God and set out—family, flocks, herds, servants and all. He headed southwest into another pagan land, called Canaan. There the Lord promised him:

"To your descendants I will give this land."

(Genesis 12:7)*

In the years that followed, Abraham journeyed up and down Canaan. He even went into Egypt for a time. And always he lived as a foreigner in a land that was not his own (see Hebrews 11:9). He stayed away from the cities of the Canaanites and kept to the central mountain ridges, where he could pasture his flocks in peace.

One night God made a COVENANT (G) with Abraham. This was an agreement that bound both of them together. It was an act of religion, for the very meaning of the word **religion** is the binding of man to God.

In due time God's promise began to be fulfilled. Abraham and his aged wife had a son, whose birth brought them such joy that they called him ISAAC, a name related to the Hebrew word for laughter.

A few years later, Abraham found himself facing the greatest challenge of his life.

On that particular morning, the bright rays of the rising sun brought no happiness into the old man's heart. Sadly he called two of his servants and young Isaac, the joy of his life. Then he saddled his donkey and chopped some wood. "The Lord has asked us to offer Him a sacrifice in the land of Moriah," he announced as the little group set out together.

Abraham didn't tell the whole story. God's words had been, "Take your only son Isaac, whom you love, and, on a mountain that I will point out to you, offer him as a burnt sacrifice."

Can you imagine the turmoil in Abraham's heart? He loved God; he loved Isaac. Moreover, the Lord had promised that he and Sarah would have so many descendants that they would seem as numerous as the stars—and Isaac was their only hope that the promise would be fulfilled.

Yet Abraham pressed on toward his destination. After some traveling, he saw a mountain in the distance and with sickening sureness knew that this was the place God meant.

"Stay here with the donkey, both of you," he told the servants. "The boy and I will go over there. We will worship and come back to you."

Abraham loaded the wood on Isaac's shoulders and tied it fast. He himself took up the knife and the fire, and the two set out together.

After a while, the boy broke the stillness. "Father!" he said.

"Yes, son?"

"We have the fire and the wood. But what about the sheep for the sacrifice?"

You can imagine how Abraham felt! But all he said was, "The Lord Himself will provide it, son."

And they walked on together.

On the height, Abraham set about building an altar and arranging the wood on it. Then he turned toward Isaac.... Suddenly the boy knew. After all, didn't the Canaanites offer their firstborn to the Lord in sacrifice?

Isaac was a brave boy. He let his father tie him up (how those old hands must have trembled!), lift him with a tremendous effort, and lay him on top of the wood.

Abraham reached for the knife.

"Abraham! Abraham!"

Was it an angel? Was it the Lord Himself?

"Yes, Lord," Abraham answered.

"Don't lay a hand on the boy. Don't do anything to him. Now I know how devoted you are to God, since you haven't refused me the son you love so much."

It had been a test of Abraham's loyalty to God—of his faith and trust. And how well he had come

14

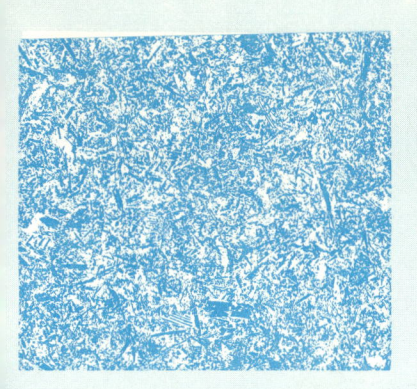

through it! His hands now trembling with joy, the old man untied his son. We can imagine Isaac leaping into his father's arms!

Abraham spied a ram whose horns had gotten tangled in a bush, so he took it and sacrificed it on the altar in the place of his son. And the Lord renewed His promise of descendants as numerous as the stars in the sky and the grains of sand on the seashore. "All the nations of the earth shall bless themselves by your descendants," God declared, "as a reward for your obedience."

Generation after generation, Abraham's descendants would hand on this story of their father's faith and obedience. From it they would learn what wholehearted dedication God deserves. They would also grasp another important fact: God does not want human sacrifices.

Yet, while the Lord does not desire such sacrifices (and, in fact, forbids them), He, instead, sent **His** only Son, whom He loves beyond all telling, to sacrifice Himself for us. O mystery of God's saving love!

Up and down the land of Canaan, Abraham built altars to the Lord, the true God. Faith and worship are duties that all of us have towards God, and even though Abraham had never heard the term "first commandment," he understood this, for he paid attention to the law of God that was written in his heart. Can you remember what God asks us to do and not do in the first commandment?

Suggested Readings: Genesis 12:1-7; 13:14-17; 22:1-19

Why is Abraham important in the history of salvation?
 Abraham is important for several reasons. He was the ancestor of the Old-Testament chosen people, who were to experience God's saving actions down through the centuries. From them would come the Savior. Abraham is also an example of total dedication to God, of faith, of trust, of obedience.

The Lord is just in all his ways
 and holy in all his works.
The Lord is near to all who call upon him,
 to all who call upon him in truth.
He fulfills the desire of those who fear him,
 he hears their cry and saves them.

(Psalm 145:17-19)*

4 RESCUE!

When Abraham's son, Isaac, grew up, he married a young woman named Rebekah. The couple had twin boys—Esau, the firstborn, and JACOB, through whom God was to continue fulfilling His promises. (God freely chooses the persons He wants to cooperate with Him in carrying out His plans.) Abraham, Isaac and Jacob are called the PATRIARCHS, or forefathers, of the Old Testament chosen people.

God changed Jacob's name to Israel. Israel's twelve sons—Reuben, Simeon, Levi, Judah, Zebulun, Issachar, Dan, Gad, Asher, Naphtali, Joseph and Benjamin—were to be the ancestors of the famous tribes of Israel.

The story of Jacob's son JOSEPH is one of the best known in the whole Old Testament. Sold into slavery by his brothers because of jealousy, Joseph was taken to Egypt, where he became highly regarded because he was good living and wise. After God had enlightened him to warn Pharaoh of an approaching drought, the young man was raised to the second highest position in Egypt and given charge of storing up provisions against the time of famine. (This remarkable rise of a "foreigner" is more easily understood when we know that the pharaohs of that period were foreigners **themselves**—Hyksos invaders who had seized power in Egypt.)

When Jacob-Israel and his eleven remaining sons found themselves in danger of starving to death, ten of the brothers went down to Egypt to buy grain. Joseph revealed himself to them (after testing their love for their father and youngest brother) and forgave them. Both Pharaoh and he invited the whole clan of Israel to come to Egypt and settle in the Nile Delta, which they did.

Joseph's story is a beautiful lesson in forgiving others. It also gives us an example of God's loving care:

"I am your brother Joseph whom you sold into Egypt. But now, do not grieve, do not reproach yourselves for having sold me here, since God sent me before you to preserve your lives."
(Genesis 45:4-5)**

Looking back at those distant times, we can see that God was working through people and events to fulfill His promises to Abraham.

In the Nile Delta the ISRAELITES (G) multiplied and prospered until about 1570 B.C., when the real Egyptians overthrew their foreign rulers. Fearing that the Israelites would revolt, the Egyptians soon enslaved them. Yet by God's providence (G) one of their number was raised in Pharaoh's own household and received a fine education, which fitted him well for the mission (G) that God would give him. This man was MOSES, who probably carried out his great work in the thirteenth century B.C.

God's call came to Moses at Mount Horeb, or Sinai, south of the land of Canaan. At that time, Moses was living in the desert as a wandering shepherd. He had married a young woman from the land of Midian, near the Gulf of Aqabah.

On that particular day so important in salvation history, Moses spied a flame leaping and dancing in the center of a bush. He watched with interest. There was no sign of anyone around, but what made him most curious was the bush itself. Instead of burning down to ashes, it kept on blazing brightly.

Marveling, Moses began to move toward the unusual sight. Then he heard (or "felt"? — at any rate, he **experienced**) a voice.

"Moses, Moses!"
"Here I am."

"Come no nearer. Take off your shoes, for the place on which you stand is holy ground. I am the God of your father...the God of Abraham, the God of Isaac and the God of Jacob."

(Exodus 3:5-6)**

As Moses covered his face in reverence and fear, God spoke on, asking him to lead all the descendants of Abraham out of Egypt and into the land He would give them — Canaan.

Moses hesitated. How could **he** go to Pharaoh and ask him to let the Israelites leave Egypt?

"I will be with you," God replied. These words were a guarantee of success. We find them again and again in the Old Testament, and history shows that God truly **was** with each person whom He encouraged in this way. Jesus would say the same to His apostles, regarding the Church. (See Matthew 28:20.)

But Moses thought of another difficulty: How would the Israelites themselves react to this?

Then Moses said to God, "I am to go, then, to the sons of Israel and say to them, 'the God of your fathers has sent me to you.' But if they ask me what his name is, what am I to tell them?" And God said to Moses, "I Am who I Am. This," he added, "is what you must say to the sons of Israel: 'I Am has sent me to you.'" And God also said to Moses, "You are to say to the sons of Israel: 'Yahweh, the God of your fathers, the God of Abraham, the God of Isaac, and the God of Jacob, has sent me to you.' This is my name for all time...."

(Exodus 3:13-15)**

No matter how these words are interpreted, they contain a wealth of meaning. "I am who I am" suggests that there is really **no** name suitable for God—no name that really describes Him. Another translation of this phrase—"I am who am"*—suggests that only God is Life itself, with everything else dependent upon Him. And from the Church's teachings we know that all this is true.

YAHWEH may be interpreted as "He causes to be" or "He is." It is the most familiar to us of all the Old Testament names for God. The Israelites themselves were to respect this name so highly that they would seldom use it. To show reverence for God's Name is one of our basic duties.

It was a great revelation that God had just given to Moses. But this first conversation of theirs dealt with other matters, too. Yahweh told the future leader what he should say to Pharaoh (that the Israelites wanted to worship their God in the desert) and what he should do if Pharaoh were stubborn. Yahweh promised to work miracles through Moses. He told him that Aaron (who was Moses' brother and a better speaker) would speak to Pharaoh for him.

So Moses returned to Egypt—a man with a mission.

It wasn't an easy mission. Pharaoh kept refusing to let the Israelites go. The miraculous transformation of a walking staff into a snake didn't impress him. Neither did the first nine plagues—natural disasters that damaged crops, harmed livestock, and disturbed the rhythm of daily life. Pharaoh knew that the waters of the Nile mysteriously turned blood red at a certain season; he also knew that his sunny land was periodically darkened by blinding sandstorms of two or three days' duration and that frogs, mosquitoes and locusts were frequent invaders of fields and homes. So when all these things occurred, one after another at Moses' command, Pharaoh paid little attention.

But—God told Moses—the plagues were just an introduction to the great act of rescue. Yahweh wanted the Israelites to see that their God was the only **true** God, and He would show this in a powerful way.

Moses' last meeting with Pharaoh was charged with tension. Weary of the Israelites' requests, Pharaoh exclaimed, "Out of my sight! If you ever appear before me again, you shall die!" And Moses, enlightened by God, retorted that all the firstborn of the Egyptians were about to die. Thus would Yahweh show His power.

It was a spring evening, and darkness had already fallen. Inside each Israelite home, families were eating a lamb or kid goat that had been offered to God in sacrifice. Some of the blood from the sacrificed victim (G) had been sprinkled on the doorposts and crosspiece over the door.

All this was a very ancient custom, to which Yahweh had chosen to give new meaning. Every home whose doorposts and lintel (crosspiece) were marked with the blood of the victim would be safe that night. This was the dread night when death prowled through the land of Egypt.

PASSOVER is our English name for the feast that the Israelites were celebrating. God asked His people to celebrate it every year. The feast's name in Hebrew (G) is very ancient and its meaning uncertain. But our English word "Passover" helps us to recall the "passing over" of the agent of death on that famous night in Egypt.

Still later the Christian feast of Easter (celebrated during the same season) would recall Jesus' passing through death to a new and risen life after His sacrifice as the true paschal lamb (G).

"**G**o, leave my people at once," Pharaoh told Moses and Aaron, whom he had sent for in the middle of the night. "And take the Israelites with you!"

Yahweh had shown His strength. Unless Pharaoh changed his mind, the sons of Israel could set out for the desert! Fearful that death might strike again, the Egyptians hurried the sons of Israel on their way and even gave them the gold and silver which God had told them to ask for.

Wives, children, livestock, belongings—the Israelites took everyone and everything along. And they marched out of Egypt dressed as if they were going to battle.

Suggested Readings: Genesis 45:1-20; 46:28-30; Exodus 1:22–2:10; 2:23–3:15

What does "Yahweh" mean?

Yahweh is one of the names for God used in the Old Testament. It may mean "He causes to be" or "He is."

What is the Passover?

The Passover of Moses' time was an ancient springtime feast, to which God gave a new meaning when He freed the Israelites in Egypt. From that day to this, it has been a memorial (a recalling or reliving) of the chosen people's liberation from slavery.

Sing Yahweh a new song!
Sing to Yahweh, all the earth!
Sing to Yahweh, bless his name.

Proclaim his salvation day after day,
tell of his glory among the nations,
tell his marvels to every people.

Let the heavens be glad, let earth rejoice,
let the sea thunder and all that it holds,
let the fields exult and all that is in them,
let all the woodland trees cry out for joy,

at the presence of Yahweh, for he comes,
he comes to judge the earth,
to judge the world with justice
and the nations with his truth.

(Psalm 96:1-3; 11-13)**

5 THE FLAMING MOUNTAIN

The Israelites were frantic. Before them lay a wide stretch of water, which could be forded with difficulty, if at all. Behind them rose a rapidly-approaching dust cloud, bright with the light of the setting sun. Surely Pharaoh's army was coming in pursuit, and here stood the sons of Israel — trapped!

"Why did you do this to us?" the people cried out to Moses. "Weren't there any burial places in Egypt? Did you have to bring us out here to die in the desert?"

"Don't be afraid," Moses told them. "If you stand fast, you'll see what a victory Yahweh will win for you today. You will never look upon these Egyptians again. God Himself will fight for you. All you need to do is keep still."

The Israelites suddenly noticed that the pillar of cloud which had been leading them on their journey — a sign of God's presence — was changing its position. As night fell with desert suddenness, the cloud placed itself between the Israelites and the approaching Egyptians, who would surely make camp now and wait for daybreak.

Moses stretched his hand out over the Sea of Reeds, and Yahweh made a strong east wind spring up. All night long it blew, driving the waters off the place where the Israelites were to cross.

When the sons of Israel saw what was happening, they lost no time. In the pre-dawn darkness, they pulled down one tent after another, loading them and their other possessions on their wagons, their animals and themselves. Then the Israelites hurried "through the sea" on that welcome strip of land!

Dawn found Moses and his people standing safe on the other shore, while the Egyptians drove their chariots toward the sea in furious pursuit. At God's command, Moses again stretched his hand out over the sea. The wind fell. Slowly yet steadily, the waters came back. Chariot wheels became clogged by mud, and as horses and drivers struggled to reach either shore, the waters grew deeper and deeper, until....

A cheer went up from the Israelite ranks. No one could complain against Moses **today**! He was a hero! And Yahweh truly **was** their God! He and His servant Moses had set them free.

Moses' sister Miriam took up a tambourine and began to chant:

"Sing to the Lord, for he is
gloriously triumphant;
horse and chariot he has
cast into the sea."
(Exodus 15:21)*

The whole community began to sing in praise of God's saving power. Their rescue had been completed. They were free!

The journey of the Israelites to Canaan is known as the EXODUS. It lasted many years.

Yahweh — who showed His presence by a column of cloud that flashed fire at night — first led the people toward the most remote region of the peninsula. There He was to tell them what He expected of them, for their ideas of Him were very confused. There, too, He would begin to make **a people** of them, for they really weren't united yet. After all, Egypt was the only home they had ever known, and not all of them

22

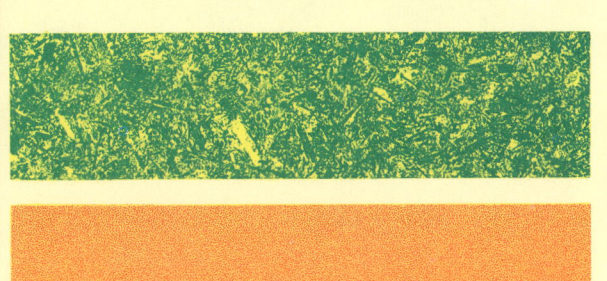

were full-blooded Israelites, either. (Quite possibly, some of these former slaves weren't Israelites at all.) Because of all this, God had not led the people along the direct, well-traveled road to Canaan, where they would surely have had to do battle with Egyptians or Canaanites. Yahweh knew that if faced with the prospect of fighting, the people would simply choose to return to slavery. They weren't ready to conquer Canaan.

On the desert march toward Mount Horeb, or Sinai, God provided the travelers with food and drink. For example, He commanded Moses to strike a rock with his staff. Immediately a spring of water gushed forth.

The food called MANNA appeared daily. Perhaps this manna was the same dew-like substance that can be found on the ground beneath tamarisk thickets on the Sinai Peninsula today. But during the Exodus it appeared in really miraculous quantities — enough to sustain thousands of people daily, with a double portion to be gathered on Fridays because of the Sabbath (Saturday) rest.

The manna was called "bread from heaven," because it came from God's loving providence (G). Centuries later, Jesus would speak of it and explain that He Himself is the true bread from heaven. (See John 6:51.)

Exclamations of excitement rippled through the Israelite camp, as the first streaks of dawn began to appear. It was the third day that they had been waiting here on the barren plain facing Mount Sinai. **This** was the day that Moses had told them to prepare for. Yahweh was about to show the people His power over nature before He entered into a covenant (G) with them.

Upon the Israelites' arrival at Sinai, the Lord had given Moses this message for the people:

"If you hearken to my voice and keep my covenant, you shall be my special possession, dearer to me than all other people, though all the earth is mine. You shall be to me a kingdom of priests, a holy nation."

(Exodus 19:5-6)*

"We will do everything the Lord has said," the people replied.

And now, at dawn on the third day, the Israelites wondered what would happen next.

Suddenly God showed His might:

There were peals of thunder on the mountain and lightning flashes, a dense cloud, and a loud trumpet blast, and inside the camp all the people trembled. Then Moses led the people out of the camp to meet God; and they stood at the bottom of the mountain. The mountain of Sinai was entirely wrapped in smoke, because Yahweh had descended on it in the form of fire. Like smoke from a furnace the smoke went up, and the whole mountain shook violently. Louder and louder grew the sound of the trumpet. Moses spoke, and God answered him with peals of thunder.
(Exodus 19:16-19)**

In another book of the Bible, Moses would be spoken of as reminding the Israelites of that great event in these words:

"The mountain flamed to the very sky....
"On the mountain, from the heart of the fire, Yahweh spoke to you face to face, and I stood all the time between Yahweh and yourselves to tell you of Yahweh's words, for you were afraid of the fire and had not gone up the mountain."
(Deuteronomy 4:11; 5:4-5)**

What did Yahweh say to the Israelites through Moses? He promised to protect them, as a good ruler protects the people he governs or as a good father protects his child. In return, He asked the Israelites to keep the ten commandments and other special laws suited to their particular time and place. The COVENANT would be the agreement between God and Israel to live up to all this.

The TEN COMMANDMENTS were a landmark in the history of morality (right living). Other nations in Moses' time already had laws, but their laws did not point out that a crime against one's fellowman is a crime against God. The ten commandments showed this. They were simple in what they said, but we know that each simple statement contains a rich meaning. This meaning would become clearer for God's chosen people down through their history, and Jesus Himself was to give the commandments their "finishing touches." He made them perfect.

The people made their promise:

"We will do everything that the Lord has told us."

(Exodus 24:3)*

Then Moses built an altar and had animals sacrificed on it. Next, he took half of the blood from the victims (G), and sprinkled it on the altar. The altar stood for Yahweh, and the blood stood for life. He took the rest of the blood and sprinkled it on the people. This showed that God and the people were joined together with a tie as strong as blood kinship, and also that the people were joined to one another.

The expression "blood of the old covenant" refers to this event. When Jesus made the "new and **everlasting**" covenant between God and man, the blood sacrificed was His own blood. Every time we receive Communion at Mass (the renewal of Jesus' sacrifice), we are joined to God in an even closer way than the Israelites were, because we receive Jesus Himself. And, being all joined to God, we are joined to one another.

Suggested Readings: Exodus 14:5-31; 16:13-31; Deuteronomy 5:6-21; Exodus 24:3-8

What was the Exodus?
The Exodus was the journey of the Israelites out of Egypt and through the desert to the "promised land"—Canaan.

What was the Sinai covenant?
The Sinai covenant was an agreement between God and the Israelites. God would protect them as His special people if they would obey the ten commandments and other laws that He gave them.

"I will sing to the Lord, for he is gloriously triumphant;
  horse and chariot he has cast into the sea.
My strength and my courage is the Lord,
  and he has been my savior.
He is my God, I praise him;
  the God of my father, I extol him.
The Lord is a warrior,
  Lord is his name!
Pharaoh's chariots and army he hurled into the sea;
  the elite of his officers were submerged in the Red Sea....
Who is like to you among the gods, O Lord?
  Who is like to you, magnificent in holiness?
O terrible in renown, worker of wonders,
  when you stretched out your right hand, the earth swallowed them!"

(Exodus 15:1-4; 11-12)*

6
PRIESTLY PEOPLE

After the making of the covenant, Moses again went up the mountain. He left Aaron and another Israelite in charge of the camp. Imagine Moses' reaction when he returned many days later and found the Israelites celebrating wildly in front of a calf made out of the gold they had received from the Egyptians! (Statues of young bulls were common idols among certain pagans. But Yahweh had forbidden His people to represent Him in this way and to worship idols.)

Moses was carrying two stone tablets upon which the commandments were engraved (the usual way of recording laws). He felt so hurt and angry because of the people's offense to God that he threw the tablets down and broke them. This symbolized the fact that the people had broken the covenant.

Moses melted the calf, ground it to powder, scattered the powder on the stream that flowed down Mount Sinai, and made the people drink. And then he begged God to forgive the Israelites for what they had done.

Because of Moses' prayer, Yahweh forgave His people renewed His covenant with them.

The covenant made the Israelites God's CHOSEN PEOPLE. We still use this name today when speaking of the Hebrews (G) of the Old Testament. They had been chosen by God as the people from whom the Savior would be born.

In the desert the chosen people became a sort of "church"—a worshiping community. Yahweh called them a "kingdom of priests" to show that they would be consecrated (dedicated) to Him in a special way. Out of this "priestly people," certain men of Moses' tribe—the tribe of Levi—were chosen to be true priests—that is, to offer sacrifice to God. The first Israelite priests were Aaron and his sons. In a special ceremony, Moses clothed Aaron with priestly vestments, which God had told him to have made. The other men of the tribe of Levi—called Levites—became the priests' helpers.

Worship consisted in various kinds of sacrifices, offered on a large altar inside a fenced-in enclosure. Also inside the enclosure was the "tabernacle," or meeting tent, containing the ARK OF THE COVENANT. The ark was made by the Israelites according to the directions God had given to Moses. It was a wooden chest, plated with gold, containing the (second) set of stone tablets into which the commandments had been engraved. On top of it was a gold throne, the "mercy seat," with carved cherubim (G) at both ends.

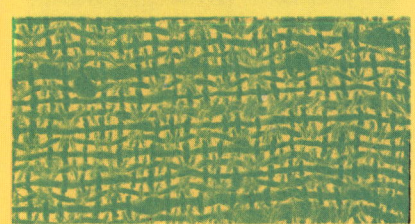

Everything was made in such a way that it could be carried from one camp site to another all the time that the Israelites were traveling through the desert.

After the ark and tent had been made, the cloud that had been leading the Israelites settled on the tent and filled it—a sign of God's presence.

The Israelites dedicated one day of the week to the Lord in a special way. This day was the SABBATH, or Saturday. (The early Christians replaced Saturday with Sunday, because Jesus rose from the dead on a Sunday.) On the Sabbath no one was to work. God made this wise law for several reasons—such as to give the people time to think about Him and the purpose of their lives, and to make sure that they had the rest which everyone needs. We, too, are not to do unnecessary hard, heavy work on "the Lord's Day" (Sunday). And God also asks us to worship Him in a special way on Sunday by taking part in the Mass—Jesus' renewal of His sacrifice. We Christians, too, are a priestly people, whom God asks to become holy.

"Yes, we can!"
"No, we can't!"
A great disagreement rocked the Israelite camp at Kadesh, an oasis many miles north of Mount Sinai and quite near to the land of Canaan.

The whole community was gathered around a small group—Moses, Aaron, and twelve men who had just come back from spying on the various peoples who lived in Canaan.

"Those peoples are too strong for us," ten of the scouts declared. "We **can't** attack them."

"Surely we should," said another scout, named Caleb. "We can do it easily." Joshua, who was the Israelites' general, agreed with Caleb.

So the community resembled a boiling kettle, and some of the people felt so discouraged that they talked about turning back. "Let's choose a leader and return to Egypt," they said.

Moses went to the meeting tent to listen to the Lord. As he had expected, Yahweh was greatly offended by those who talked of returning to Egypt, for they showed no trust in Him, their God. Although Yahweh **did** forgive His people, He promised that none of those who had wanted to rebel would live to see the Israelites' entrance into Canaan. "To the last man," He said, "they shall die here in the desert."

This was the reason for the chosen people's long stay in the desert, most of which was spent at the oasis of Kadesh. By the time the Israelites again set out for Canaan (taking a roundabout route), a whole new generation had grown up and everyone who had wanted to return to Egypt was dead. In all, the chosen people spent about forty years in the desert before they entered Canaan. This period of waiting was good for them, because they learned to obey God and to trust in His providence, which He kept showing them in all their needs.

Soon after the community finally set out from Kadesh, Yahweh told Moses that Aaron was about to die. At God's command, Moses and Aaron climbed up Mount Hor, taking along Eleazar, Aaron's eldest surviving son. There on the mountain, Moses took his brother's priestly vestments and put them on Eleazar, the community's new priest. Aaron died there, and the whole community mourned for him for thirty days.

Moses, too, was to die before the Israelites entered the promised land. He knew it, for God had told both him and Aaron beforehand. At one point in their journey thay had sinned against the Lord. The Bible does not clearly state what they did, and different people give different explanations about it. But we **do** know that they failed God in some way.

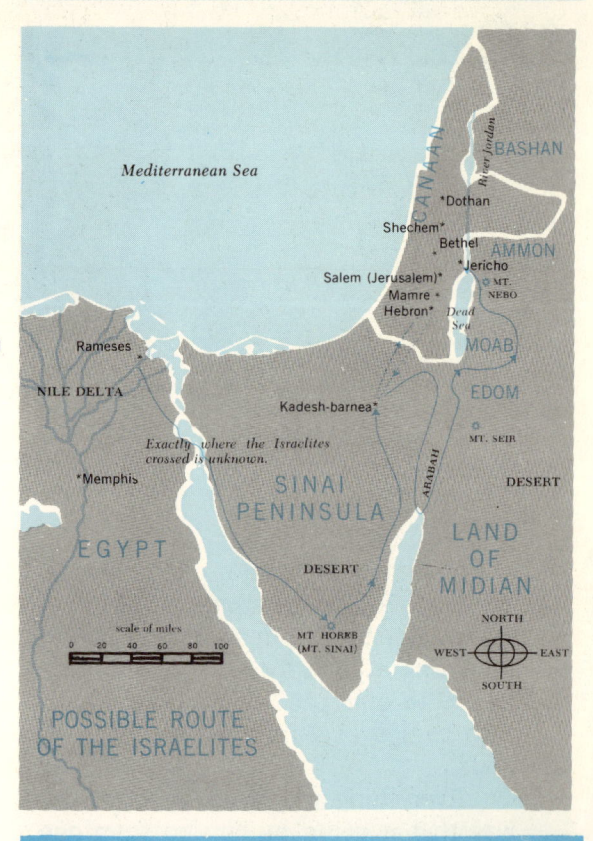

Therefore, after the Israelites had reached the eastern border of Canaan, Yahweh told Moses to pass his leadership on to JOSHUA. Moses did so, in the presence of all the people. He had already reminded them:

"Listen, Israel: Yahweh our God is the one Yahweh. You shall love Yahweh your God with all your heart, with all your soul, with all your strength. Let these words I urge on you today be written on your heart...."

"When Yahweh has brought you into the land which he swore to your fathers Abraham, Isaac and Jacob that he would give you, with great and prosperous cities not of your building, houses full of good things not furnished by you, wells you did not dig, vineyards and olives you did not plant, when you have eaten these and had your fill, then take care you do not forget Yahweh who brought you out of the land of Egypt, out of the house of slavery. You must fear Yahweh your God, you must serve him."

(Deuteronomy 6:4-6, 10-13)**

Moses died on Mount Nebo in the land of Moab, from which he could see far into the promised land. The chosen people mourned for him for thirty days; then Joshua made ready to lead them across the River Jordan into Canaan.

Suggested Readings: Exodus 32:1-24, 30-34; Deuteronomy 31:7-8; 34:1-9

How did the events of the Exodus and Mount Sinai change the Israelites?
    The Israelites became united into a real people—God's "chosen people," a worshiping community which learned to obey and trust Him.

Let God arise, let his enemies be scattered,
let those who hate him flee before him!
God, when you set out at the head of your people,
and marched across the desert, the earth rocked,
the heavens deluged at God's coming,
at the coming of God, the God of Israel.
God, you rained a downpour of blessings,
when your heritage was faint you gave it strength;
your family found a home, where you
in your goodness, God, provided for the needy.
Blessed be the Lord day after day,
the God who saves us and bears our burdens!

(Psalm 68:1, 7-10, 19)**

29

Unit 2 Toward the Fullness of Time

7 LAND OF THE PROMISE

It was spring, and the waters of the Jordan River were swollen from winter rains and the melting snows of Mount Hermon. Yet as Joshua led his people toward the river, he was confident of crossing. Yahweh had assured him of His help.

Joshua told the Israelites, "The ark of the covenant of the Lord of the whole earth will enter the Jordan ahead of you. When the feet of the priests who carry the ark touch the water, it will stop flowing."

And so it happened. The priests marched into the Jordan, carrying the ark. And the waters began to drop steadily until the riverbed was bare. No more waters were flowing down from upstream. To those of the Israelites who had crossed through the Reed Sea, it was the same great event all over again!

The priests carrying the ark stood in the riverbed until all the people had crossed. Then they, too, climbed up the bank into Canaan. And the Jordan began to flow again. The waters rose until the river began to flood the shore, as before.

Just as Yahweh had helped the Israelites leave Egypt by sweeping the sea bed clear with a strong wind, so He may have used a landslide farther upstream to halt the Jordan's waters long enough for the chosen people to cross. Such landslides take place in the Jordan valley every once in a while. If this was what Yahweh used, He timed it perfectly!

Camping on the plains of Jericho, the Israelites celebrated the Passover. That same day, the manna ceased, for God's people were able to gather and eat the grain of the land of Canaan.

Canaan, however, had to be taken by force. The first city that stood in the Israelites' path was Jericho.

We know from the Book of Joshua that the Israelites **took** Jericho through the help of God. The biblical account tells us that Yahweh's power caused the walls protecting the city to collapse. Archaeologists have tried to learn more about this. But although they have uncovered the ruins of a very ancient Jericho, they have not found those of a thirteenth-century-B.C. city. Some people think that the Israelites seized the more ancient city, already partly destroyed; others believe that the remains of Joshua's Jericho have been washed away by the yearly rains or swept off by the wind.

Leaving the ark of the covenant at Gilgal, Joshua and his fighting men pushed farther into Canaan. They fought and were defeated, fought again and won....

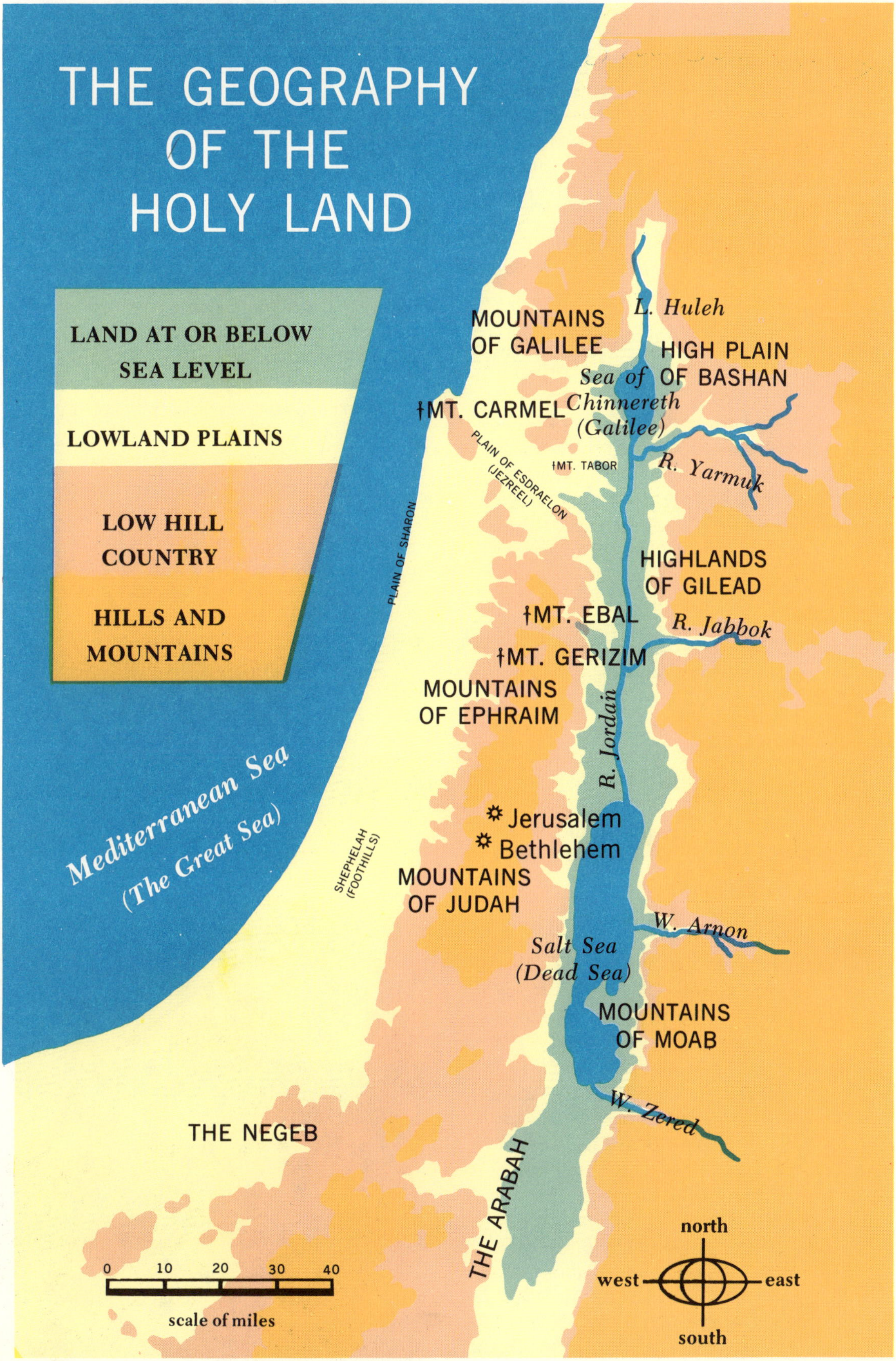

THE GEOGRAPHY OF THE HOLY LAND

Legend:
- LAND AT OR BELOW SEA LEVEL
- LOWLAND PLAINS
- LOW HILL COUNTRY
- HILLS AND MOUNTAINS

MOUNTAINS OF GALILEE
L. Huleh
HIGH PLAIN OF BASHAN
†MT. CARMEL
Sea of Chinnereth (Galilee)
PLAIN OF SHARON
PLAIN OF ESDRAELON (JEZREEL)
†MT. TABOR
R. Yarmuk
HIGHLANDS OF GILEAD
†MT. EBAL
†MT. GERIZIM
R. Jabbok
MOUNTAINS OF EPHRAIM
R. Jordan
Mediterranean Sea (The Great Sea)
SHEPHELAH (FOOTHILLS)
✲ Jerusalem
✲ Bethlehem
MOUNTAINS OF JUDAH
W. Arnon
Salt Sea (Dead Sea)
MOUNTAINS OF MOAB
W. Zered
THE NEGEB
THE ARABAH

scale of miles: 0 10 20 30 40

north / west — east / south

During Joshua's second military campaign, a famous and (to us) mysterious event took place. The Israelites had been called to help their allies, the people of Gibeon, whose city was being attacked by five Amorite kings. Joshua led his men in an all-night march and caught the Amorites by surprise. But he needed God's help to win the battle, so he prayed for the sun and moon to stand still. The language is poetic; it might remind us of someone wishing that a clock would temporarily stop. At any rate, Joshua was asking for God's help, and he received it in the form of thick clouds and a hailstorm, which refreshed the weary night-marchers while it slowed down the fleeing Amorites. (Because of the poetic form of writing that the Bible uses at this point, it doesn't seem that the earth actually stopped turning on its axis.)

It was a smashing victory. After this, Joshua pushed farther south and conquered other cities. Then he launched a third campaign throughout northern Canaan. Again it was a success, as the Bible tells us. For example, the Book of Joshua speaks of the destruction of a very important city named Hazor. Archaeologists have found the burned ruins of this city and of several others — all destroyed about the same time.

Within about fifty years of the Israelites' entrance into the promised land, most of Canaan's cities had been conquered. Others (such as Jerusalem) were to hold out longer — even through the two-hundred-year period of the "judges."

Among the causes of the Israelites' success were these: first, Yahweh's direct help. Then, the Canaanites' lack of unity. Each city was pretty much on its own, whereas the Israelites attacked as a united force. Another cause was God's timing of the Israelite conquest, for Joshua led his troops into Canaan from the east around the time that the Philistines (island peoples from the Aegean Sea) began to settle in the west and push inland. Most of the surviving Canaanites fled north into Phoenicia.

During Joshua's lifetime Canaan was divided up among the twelve tribes. The names of these tribes were almost the same as those of Jacob-Israel's twelve sons, but not quite. Jacob had adopted Joseph's sons, Ephraim and Manasseh, as his own, so the tribes with these names took the place of what would have been "the tribe of Joseph." This made thirteen tribes, but the Levites — chosen by God to be the priests and their helpers — were given certain cities throughout the land instead of a single large piece of territory.

What sort of land was divided among the tribes? A land of fertile, green valleys and mountain pastures, a land of fruitful olive plantations and desolate deserts, a land that was both poor and rich because of its particular geography. In Canaan the Israelites could choose to tend flocks on the hills, raise crops in the valleys or carry on trade.

After the land had been divided, Joshua called his people together at Shechem to renew the covenant. Yahweh's covenant with the chosen people was a matter of personal dedication, just as Baptism has to be for each one of us. Most of these Israelites had been born after the events of Mount Sinai. Because of the covenant, they truly **were** God's people, but they needed to show that they were aware of this fact. A boy or girl who prepares for Confirmation is doing much the same thing.

The period that followed Joshua's conquest is called the time of the JUDGES. Israel was now a **nation,** because at last the chosen people had a land of their own. But Israel had no human king, as other nations did. **Yahweh** was the king, and what united the people was the ark of the covenant, which was kept at Shiloh, an important city near the center of the country.

The history of God's people at this time falls into a pattern that keeps repeating itself. Whenever some of the Israelites would forsake Yahweh and worship Baal (the god of the Canaanites), Yahweh would withdraw His help and allow an enemy to conquer some or all of the land. Then there would be cries of sorrow and prayers for help. Seeing the people's repentance, Yahweh would forgive them and inspire a military leader—called a judge—to free Israel from its enemies. This happened time and again.

The judges weren't always models of right-living. The strong SAMSON, for example, fell into sins against

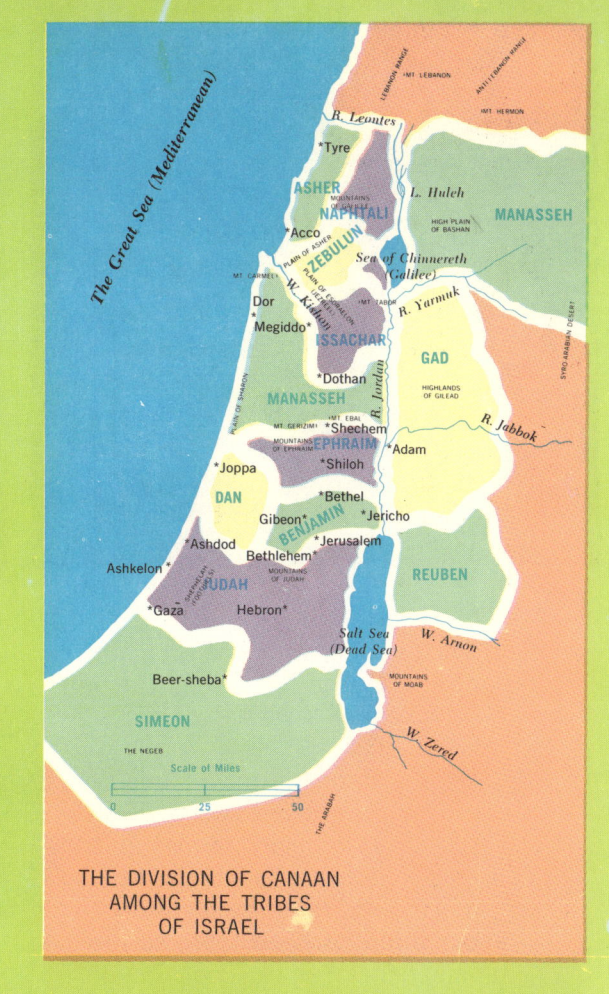

THE DIVISION OF CANAAN AMONG THE TRIBES OF ISRAEL

the sixth commandment and was captured by the Philistines through the trickery of a woman.

One of the most famous of the judges was GIDEON—an ordinary farmer and the father of a family. At God's command, he reduced his army to about three hundred men, so it would be clear that Yahweh, not Gideon, was the victor over the Midianites.

Gideon and his men surrounded an enemy camp in the dark. Each of them had a horn and an empty jar with a torch inside. When a signal was given, they all blew their horns, shouted and broke their jars. Torch in one hand, horn in the other, every Israelite soldier continued to blow and shout, while the panic-stricken Midianites began to run about wildly. In a few moments they were blindly fighting one another. When the few survivors fled in terror, the Israelites pursued them, caught up with them and put their leaders to death.

"Rule over us," the soldiers said to Gideon, "you and your son and his son—for you rescued us from the power of the Midianites."

"No, I won't rule over you," Gideon replied, "nor will my son. The **Lord** must be your ruler."

And Gideon went back to his farm.

Another famous judge was a wife and mother. The prophetess DEBORAH often told the people what God expected of them.

Two of God's promises to Abraham had been fulfilled. In the desert, the Israelites had become a people. In Canaan they had become a nation. But what about the third promise—that somehow, because of Abraham, all the nations of the earth would be blessed?

That blessing would come about through the Savior, Jesus Christ. Right after the Book of Judges, the Bible gives us the beautiful story of RUTH, one of Jesus' ancestors.

Ruth was a Moabite girl. She married Mahlon, a young Israelite from Bethlehem who had settled in Moab with his parents and brother.

Not long after the marriage, both Mahlon and his brother died. Naomi, Ruth's mother-in-law, decided to return to Bethlehem, since her husband, too, was now dead. Naomi urged Ruth to return to the Moabites. But Ruth loved her mother-in-law, who was old and had no one to support her. "Don't ask me to leave you," she said.

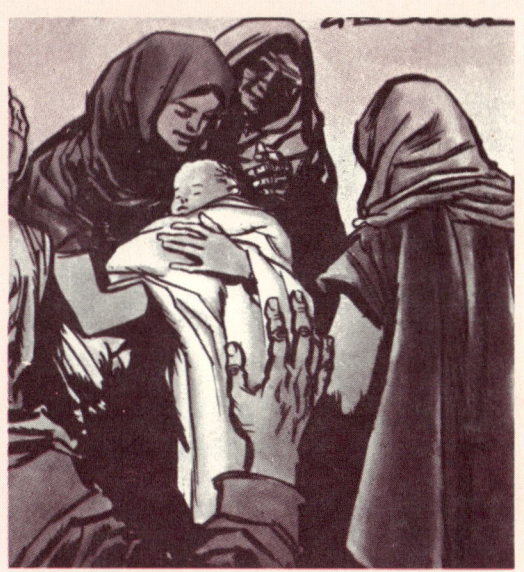

> "Wherever you go, I will go, wherever you live, I will live. Your people shall be my people, and your God, my God."
>
> (Ruth 1:16)**

So when Naomi returned to Bethlehem, her Moabite daughter-in-law went with her.

At once Ruth set to work to support them both. She asked permission to follow the servants reaping grain in a certain field, in order to gather up what they left behind. The field belonged to Boaz, a relative of her deceased husband. When Boaz met Ruth he expressed his admiration for her:

> "I have been told all you have done for your mother-in-law since your husband's death, and how you left your own father and mother and the land where you were born to come among a people whom you knew nothing about before you came here. May Yahweh reward you for what you have done!"
>
> (Ruth 2:11)**

And Yahweh **did** reward her. To Naomi's great joy, Boaz married Ruth. According to the custom of the time, their firstborn son became the legal heir of Naomi's deceased husband. Naomi had a "grandson"! The boy was named Obed. His own grandson would be one of the greatest kings of all time—David.

Suggested Readings: Joshua 24:1-28; Judges 6:1–7:22; 8:22-23; Ruth 1:1–2:23; 4:13-17

What happened after the Israelites entered Canaan?
The Israelites conquered most of the country and divided it among the twelve tribes. During the time of Joshua and the judges, they lived as a nation whose king was God Himself. God raised up judges (military leaders) to help them in time of need.

> Happy are they whose way is blameless,
>   who walk in the law of the Lord.
> Happy are they who observe his decrees,
>   who seek him with all their heart,
> And do no wrong,
>   but walk in his ways.
>
> (Psalm 119:1-3)*

8 THREE MEN AND A KINGDOM

In the first half of the eleventh century B.C., pilgrims (G) from various parts of the land would come to Shiloh, bringing animals to sacrifice in the presence of the ark of the covenant.

The priest Eli—one of Aaron's descendants—always saw familiar faces in the throng, for some of these people came every year. One particular time a woman approached him, accompanied by her little son.

"Excuse me, my Lord," she exclaimed. "I am the woman who once stood here near you, praying to Yahweh. I prayed for this child, and God has answered my prayer. Now I am giving him to Yahweh. As long as he lives, he will be dedicated to God."

Thus began the story of SAMUEL, who was to be the last of the judges and a famous PROPHET—a man who spoke for God to the people, as Moses had done.

Samuel grew up there in Shiloh, at the shrine of the ark. The times were troubled. In fact, because of the sinfulness of Eli's sons, Yahweh eventually permitted the Philistines to capture the ark and destroy Shiloh.

Even though the Philistines later returned the ark (through fear of it), they remained a constant threat to the Israelites throughout Samuel's lifetime.

At last the leaders of the people came to Samuel and asked him to anoint a king to lead them in battle. Samuel hesitated because he felt that if the people had a king they would forget about Yahweh, their **real** King. But God told him to go ahead and anoint the man He would point out.

That man was SAUL, the tall, handsome son of a well-to-do farmer. After he won a great victory over the Ammonites, the people joyfully accepted him as the king they had asked for.

A real fighter, Saul set out to war against the Philistines. And God was with him until he began to disobey the Lord's word as given to him through Samuel. "Your kingdom will not last," Samuel warned, the first time that Saul disobeyed. The second time, Samuel declared, "Since you have rejected God's command, he, too, has rejected you as ruler."

From that time on, Saul began to slide downhill. His faults began to show up. He easily became depressed and fell into fits of jealousy. To cheer him, his servants found a skilled musician—a handsome shepherd boy from Bethlehem—to play the harp for him. Saul enjoyed the boy's music, and much of the time he kept DAVID with him in his rustic fortress at Gibeah. No one in Saul's household knew that in Bethlehem Samuel had secretly anointed David as king!

Besides being a musician, David was also a fighting man. And he loved Yahweh with all his heart. When the Philistine giant Goliath challenged the Israelites to send a soldier against him in singlehanded combat, David asked Saul to send **him.** He went out against Goliath "in the name of the Lord...so the whole land may learn that Israel has a God."

David felled the giant with a stone from his shepherd's sling and then dispatched him with a stroke of Goliath's own sword.

Soon Saul and David **together** were leading Israel's army out to battle against the Philistines. Meanwhile, a firm friendship had sprung up between David and Saul's son Jonathan, while Michal, one of Saul's daughters, had fallen in love with the shepherd-warrior. All seemed to be going well for everyone until the day that Saul and David, returning from battle, were met by women joyfully shaking their tambourines and singing, "Saul has killed his thousands, David his tens of thousands."

Saul was furious. "The only thing left for him is the kingship," he thought. David must be gotten out of the way at all costs! He must be sent out into battle again and again!

But David did not die at the hands of the Philistines.

"He's dangerous," Saul told Jonathan and his servants. "He must be killed." Of course, Jonathan told David, who was on guard from then on.

One day, as the young man was playing his harp, Saul took his spear and hurled it at him. The king was a good marksman, but David moved fast. He stepped aside and fled, helped in his escape by his wife, Michal.

Jonathan tried to reason with his father, but he failed. Seeing that Saul was still determined to kill David, Jonathan met his friend at a prearranged spot and warned him how serious the situation was. They renewed their promise of lasting friendship and parted. David went back into hiding.

Saul's jealousy took him farther and farther away from God. Learning that the priests of Nob had given David food and a sword, Saul had the priests murdered. Then he gathered a band of troops and set out to pursue David (now joined by many of his kinsfolk and other fighting men), who was hiding here and there in the hilly desert of Judah.

David had some close escapes, but so did Saul. Twice the young warrior could easily have killed the king, but both times he refused to do so. After all, he thought, Israel's king was dedicated to the Lord; in fact Saul had been **chosen** by Yahweh.

David (himself chosen by Yahweh) would wait for God to act through other people and events.

And that time did indeed come. The Israelites and Philistines met in a dreadful battle at Mount Gilboa. Jonathan and two of his brothers were killed. Himself wounded, Saul committed suicide rather than fall into the hands of the enemy.

Was David glad? Far from it! Rather, he wept for:

"Saul and Jonathan, beloved and cherished,

> separated neither in life nor
>   in death,
> swifter than eagles, stronger
>   than lions!"
>
> (2 Samuel 1:23)*

After Saul's death, the tribe of Judah proclaimed David king, and he reigned over them for seven years and six months, with the southern city of Hebron as his capital. Then the other tribes, too, accepted him, and the capital was moved to a neutral location, JERUSALEM, which the king and his men captured from the Jebusites.

To Jerusalem David brought the ark of the covenant, thus making that city the religious center of the chosen people.

This was the beginning of Israel's golden age. The time was about 1000 B.C., and King David was about thirty years old when he started to reign in Jerusalem. He organized a powerful nation, which little by little subdued the Philistines. Meanwhile, having a palace of his own, he felt a need to build a temple for the ark of the Lord. However, the prophet NATHAN told him that Yahweh didn't want a temple now; the king's son, instead, would build it. And Nathan continued with a marvelous promise: David's dynasty would last forever! We can see now how true this promise was, for Jesus Christ, "Son of David," is our King now and He will be King forever.

Yet, for all David's love of God, he was not perfect. He had his human weaknesses, as everyone does. David committed a sin of adultery, and when he realized that it could not be covered up because a child was to be born, he arranged to have the woman's husband die in battle so he could take her as his own wife.

Nathan the prophet had the courage to reprove the king for his sins, and David wept bitterly when he realized how greatly God had been offended.

Several sorrows came to David toward the end of his life—including an attempted seizure of the kingdom by his son Absalom—and the king accepted these sufferings as what he deserved because of his sins. This was one of the marks of David's greatness—his humility (G). He knew that before Yahweh he was "little," for everything he had was the Lord's gift to him. The **real** king of the chosen people was Yahweh.

Suggested Readings: 1 Samuel 3:1-18; 16:1-13; 17:41-51; 26:1-25; 2 Samuel 7:1-17

How did the dynasty of David come about?

The chosen people asked for a king. Their first king, Saul, disobeyed God and was replaced by the more faithful David. David pleased the Lord so much that Yahweh promised him a dynasty that would never end.

Yahweh, remember David
and all the hardships he suffered,
and the oath he swore to Yahweh,
his vow to the Mighty One of Jacob:

not to enter tent or house,
not to climb into bed,
not to allow himself to sleep,
not even to close his eyes,
until he had found a place for Yahweh,
a home for the Mighty One of Jacob!

Yahweh, go up to your resting place,
you and your ark of power.

(Psalm 132:1-5, 8)**

9 A NATION CRUMBLES

King David was startled. He had just received word that one of his sons, Adonijah, was proclaiming himself king! And here stood Nathan the prophet, asking what should be done. Was Adonijah to take over the kingdom?

"Call Benaiah and Zadok," the aging king ordered. Benaiah was one of his most loyal fighting men; Zadok, one of the priests. As soon as Benaiah arrived, the king told him, "Take the members of the royal bodyguard and mount my son SOLOMON on my own mule. Escort him down to Gihon (a spring in the Kidron Valley). There, Zadok and Nathan, you are to anoint him king of Israel."

So Solomon was quickly led down into the valley in a solemn procession. As soon as he had been anointed, everyone shouted, "Long live King Solomon!" The young man was brought back to the royal palace amid shouts and the playing of flutes. He took his seat on the royal throne, and all the servants went to promise him their loyalty.

As he lay in his sick bed, King David breathed a sigh of relief. Solomon would make a much better king than the power-hungry Adonijah. Solomon was wiser and seemed to have more love for Yahweh....

Solomon **was** wise, and he asked the Lord for more wisdom so he could govern Israel well. Then, because the land was now at peace, he decided to bring timber from Lebanon and have a splendid TEMPLE built for the ark of the covenant. This Solomon did. The finished temple looked magnificent! So, too, did his new royal palace.

On the day of the temple's dedication, the ark of the covenant was brought into it in a solemn procession. And after the offering of countless sacrifices, a cloud entered the temple and filled it, showing God's presence, as in the days of the Exodus.

For the next three hundred seventy years, this temple was to be the center of worship in the kingdom of David's successors.

Solomon began his reign as a wise man, a man of God. But he also showed himself clever in the ways of the world. He was good at carrying on commerce and also at taxing the people. His kingdom, and especially the king himself, became wealthy.

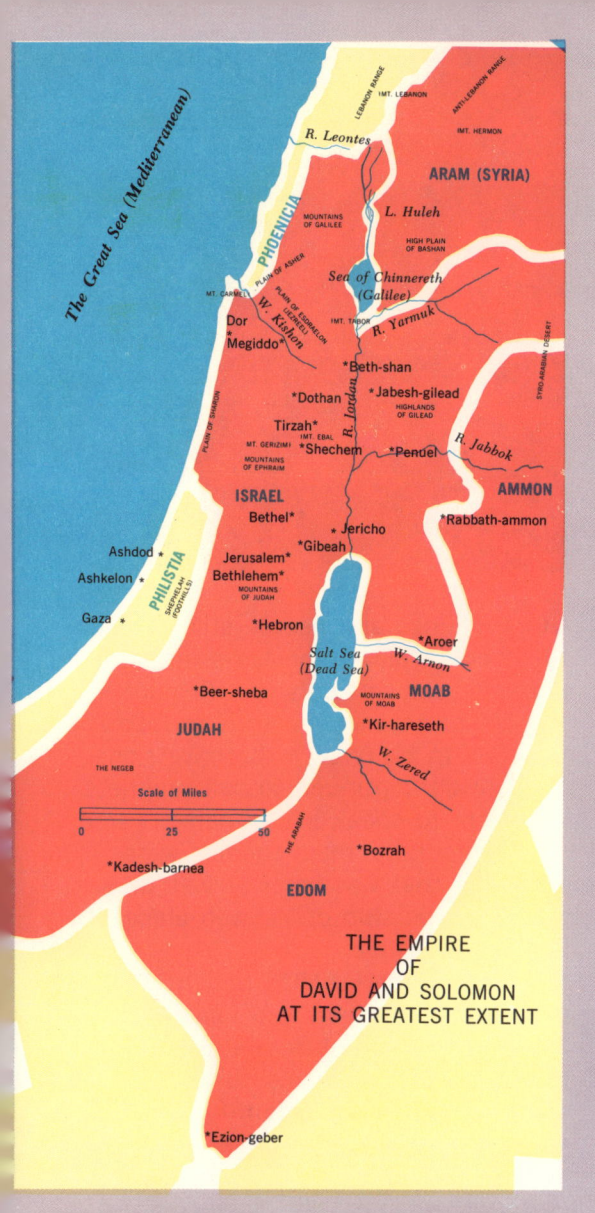

THE EMPIRE OF DAVID AND SOLOMON AT ITS GREATEST EXTENT

Moreover, he married pagan women—not just one, but one after another. These women had their own gods, and to please his wives Solomon built shrines to honor these gods. For pagans, it was nothing to worship more than one God. But for an Israelite—who knew better—even to build a shrine to another god was very wrong. The true God is "a jealous God"—just because He **is** the only God.

Thus, Israel's golden age came to an end. Yahweh told Solomon that ten of the twelve tribes would break away and form a separate kingdom. (Only the tribes of Judah and Benjamin would be left to David's descendants.)

This was exactly what happened after the king's death. The northern tribes rebelled against Solomon's son, and became a separate kingdom under Jeroboam, who had once supervised the work of Solomon's builders. The new northern kingdom kept the name ISRAEL, while the southern one was called JUDAH.

Israel soon began to turn away from Yahweh because of the gold-plated statues of bulls that Jeroboam set up in two cities. Perhaps the king intended the bulls to be regarded as pedestals on which the invisible Yahweh could stand (something like the mercy-seat throne on the ark of the covenant), but not everyone understood this. Because bull statues were connected with worship of the Canaanite god, Baal, pagan worship spread throughout the land, and with it all sorts of sinful actions.

When a prophet told Jeroboam that the altar the king had placed in front of the bull would one day be destroyed, Jeroboam ordered the prophet to be seized. But at once the king's outstretched hand withered, and he begged the man of God to pray for him. The prophet did so; the hand was restored. But Jeroboam did not change his ways.

41

THE TWO KINGDOMS—
ISRAEL AND JUDAH

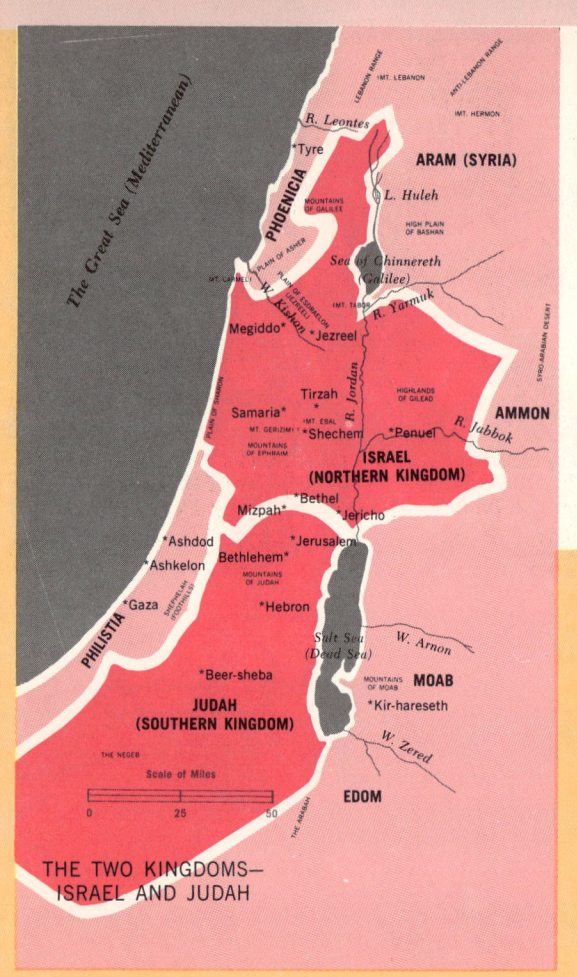

The most evil king of Israel seems to have been Ahab, whose queen was a pagan woman named Jezebel. Under them the worship of Yahweh almost died out.

But the Lord began to raise up prophets to reprove the kings and show people the way back to Him. Two great prophets in the time of Ahab and his successors (the mid-ninth century B.C.) were ELIJAH and ELISHA. Both worked miracles in Yahweh's name. In fact, some of these miracles foreshadowed those of Jesus. Right then, miracles were truly needed to turn the hearts of the Israelites back to God.

After the deaths of Ahab and Jezebel, religious conditions in the northern kingdom improved somewhat. But the kings and people still needed to be **converted**—to be led away from sin and back to God's law. (In fact, the life of **anyone** who tries to follow God has to be filled with conversions.) So Yahweh continued to call prophets, who were to speak in His name. Three of the prophets' main themes were: a religion that was **inner** as well as outer, the worship of Yahweh **alone**, and social **justice**.

The prophets AMOS and HOSEA preached in the northern kingdom around the mid-eighth century B.C. Hosea is famous for his comparison of Israel to a bride unfaithful to Yahweh, her husband. Amos condemned the oppression of the poor by the merchants, who cheated them, and by the kings, who did nothing to help them. As Jesus Himself would do, Amos told the people that it is not enough to perform religious actions; one must be religious in the heart and show it through justice and goodness.

Amos and Hosea were God's final messengers to the northern kingdom, and that kingdom refused to listen. In 721 B.C., the Assyrians conquered Israel, took most of its people into exile, and brought in pagans from other conquered lands to take their place. These people intermarried with the few surviving Israelites, picked up a bit of the religion of Yahweh, and eventually evolved into the Samaritans.

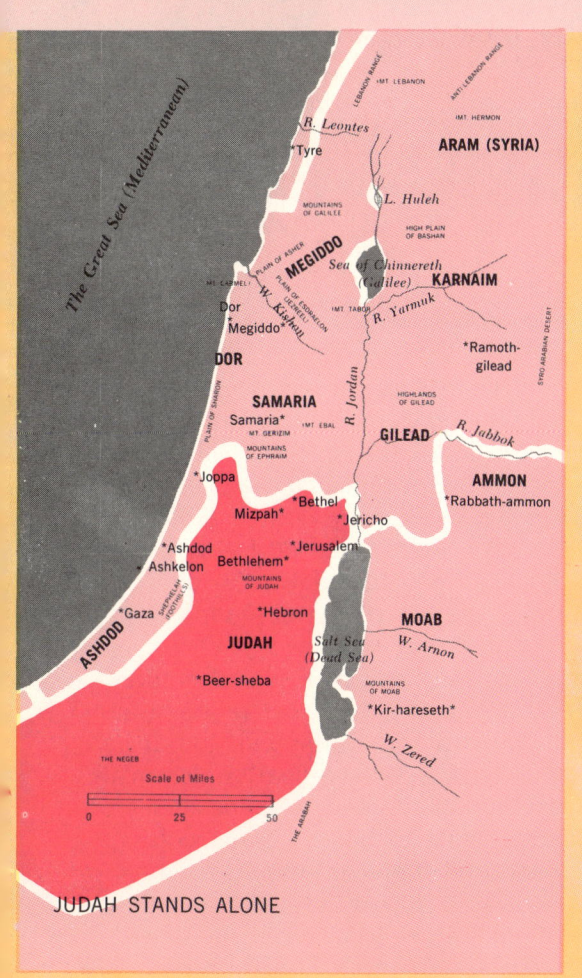

JUDAH STANDS ALONE

A young man from a priestly family tried to bring the people back to their senses. His name was JEREMIAH, and in the beginning of his ministry he was not alone in his efforts. JOSIAH, the last of Judah's really good kings, was trying to undo the harm brought about by Manasseh.

But Josiah marched out to fight against the pharaoh of Egypt (who was passing through the land) and died in battle. His four successors were not men to listen to the word of the Lord.

Shy and sensitive Jeremiah found himself repeating Yahweh's messages to deaf ears. Judah was about to be punished for its unfaithfulness to God, but no one would listen. At one point Jeremiah was scourged and put in stocks. Another time he was imprisoned in the court of the guards. Again, he was beaten and placed in a dungeon. And finally his enemies lowered him into a cistern full of mud.

But all these trials were nothing compared with his sorrow over what he knew was coming. And it came with awful sureness. In 598 B.C. the Babylonians under Nebuchadnezzar threatened Jerusalem and took some of its leading citizens into exile. Ten years later the dreadful siege began. For eighteen months the starving inhabitants of the city held out while Nebuchadnezzar's forces battered away at the fortified walls. Then Jerusalem fell.

Around the time that Israel fell, the first really good king since David was reigning in Judah. His name was HEZEKIAH, and he had the support and advice of two prophets, the brilliant ISAIAH and the obscure MICAH. Hezekiah tried to rescue survivors from the northern kingdom and carry out a religious reform—which meant bringing God's people back to the true worship of Him and the keeping of His laws.

But Hezekiah's son, Manasseh, undid all his father's good work and introduced more shameful pagan rites into Judah than had ever been practiced before. Had the lesson of the northern kingdom been forgotten? Didn't the people of Judah realize that the very same tragedy could befall them?

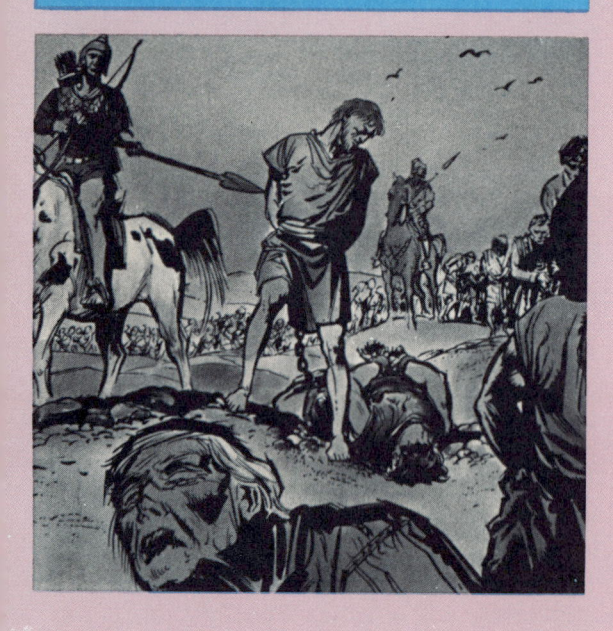

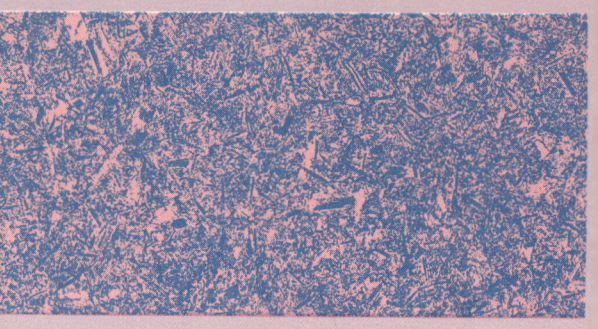

The victors sacked Solomon's temple and carried off everything valuable—all the bronze, gold and silver vessels that had been used in worship. Then they burned the temple, the royal palace and all the large buildings and tore down the city walls. The ark of the covenant disappeared and was never seen again. Except for some who sought safety in Egypt and a few poor farmers, all the survivors were taken off to Babylon in exile. The broken-hearted Jeremiah, instead, was forced by some of his countrymen to flee to Egypt with them, and there he died.

Was it all over? No. Rather, this was like a seed buried in the earth that gives rise to a sturdy young plant. Already God had raised up another prophet in Babylon. During the painful years of the BABYLONIAN EXILE, EZEKIEL was to encourage his people with the hope of a better future—a time when the Lord Himself would be king and shepherd over His "flock"—the chosen people.

Suggested Readings: 1 Kings 17:17-24; 18:20-39; Amos 8:1-7, 11-12; 2 Kings 22:1—23:3; 2 Chronicles 36:1-21

What messages did the prophets give the kings and people before the two kingdoms were destroyed?

Three main messages were: the importance of **inner** as well as outer religion, the fact that **only** the true God was to be worshiped, the need for justice and goodness towards one's fellowmen.

Save us, O Lord, our God,
  and gather us from among the nations,
That we may give thanks to your holy name
  and glory in praising you.

(Psalm 106:47)*

10 NEW CHALLENGES, NEW HEROES

> I will make you the light of the nations
> so that my salvation may reach to the ends of the earth.
> (Isaiah 49:6)**

So spoke the Lord through the pen of "Second Isaiah," an anonymous prophet writing in Babylon during the Exile. The Lord was speaking to His people, hinting that in them—as He had promised to Abraham—all the nations of the earth would be blessed.

Was this a strange saying, seeing that the kingdoms of Israel and Judah were no more, Jerusalem and the temple had been destroyed, and the ark of the covenant had vanished? Not at all, for the one thing that really mattered was happening: the people were turning back to their God.

Ezekiel's encouragement had helped them to understand two important truths. First, Yahweh was not a local god, whose presence depended on the existence of the ark and the temple. Yahweh was the Lord of the whole earth. He was everywhere, even here in Babylon with them.

Second, God would not hold His people responsible for the sins and crimes of their ancestors. Each of them could make a fresh start.

And then there was the promise: **a new exodus** would take place—a return of the exiles from Babylon. After they had been purified, after they had wholeheartedly come back to Yahweh, the chosen people would be permitted to return home!

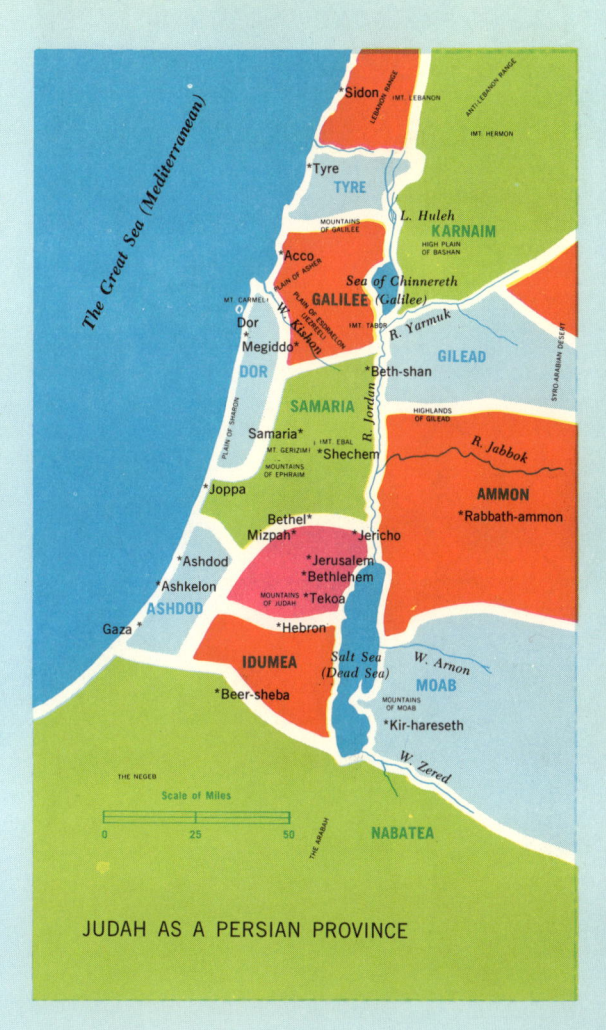

JUDAH AS A PERSIAN PROVINCE

Sang the pen of Second Isaiah:
> Yes, you will leave with joy
> and be led away in safety.
> Mountains and hills will
>   break into joyful cries
>   before you
> and all the trees of the countryside clap their hands.
> (Isaiah 55:12)**

The man whom God raised up to deliver His people was Cyrus, king of the Persians and Medes, who conquered Babylon in 539 B.C., forty-eight years after the destruction of the temple (587 B.C.). The following year, Cyrus had this decree proclaimed throughout his kingdom:

"Yahweh, the God of heaven, has given me all the kingdoms of the earth; he has ordered me to build him a Temple in Jerusalem, in Judah. Whoever there is among you of all his people, may his God be with him! Let him go up to Jerusalem in Judah to build the Temple of Yahweh, the God of Israel."

(Ezra 1:2-3)**

So some of the people began to return to their homeland. It was hard to begin again in Judah, a small, poor, ruined country, surrounded by unfriendly neighbors, such as the Samaritans and the Ammonites. So at first the people dedicated all their efforts to obtaining homes and land. Seventeen years passed, and still the temple remained in ruins. Only one attempt had been made to rebuild it, an attempt blocked by the Samaritans (G).

Then Yahweh raised up two energetic prophets, HAGGAI and ZECHARIAH. Haggai went straight to Joshua, the high priest, and Zerubbabel—one of David's descendants, whom the Persians had made governor of Jerusalem. He told them plainly that everything would go better for the people if they stopped worrying so much about their own problems and started to rebuild the house of the Lord.

Zerubbabel and Joshua listened and acted. Five years later, the new temple (although less magnificent), stood on the site of the old.

Seventy years passed. Jerusalem had a temple, yes, but no walls. One of the chosen people who held a high position in Babylon decided to do something about this. His name was NEHEMIAH, and he received the Persian king's permission to rebuild the walls of the city.

When he arrived in Jerusalem, Nehemiah recruited a whole task force of volunteers. And did they work! In a matter of months, the walls had been finished. Jerusalem need no longer fear an enemy attack.

At some point during this period following the Exile, JUDAISM began, probably under the leadership of a priest named EZRA. Judaism was the organization of Jerusalem and Judah around the temple, under the leadership of the high priest. In other words, religion and politics were mixed, but religion came first. David's descendants still lived in Judah (St. Joseph would be one of them), but they were not called kings, because the country was ruled by a foreign power. The real authority was in the hands of the high priest.

By this time much of the Old Testament had been written down, and great interest was taken in the study of the Scriptures. The study of the commandments and other laws that God had given His people was considered especially important.

As Judaism was developing, momentous events were taking place throughout the Near East. In 336 B.C. a young man named Alexander became king of Macedon. He had a dream of uniting the whole world and set out to accomplish it by force. In less than thirteen years, Alexander the Great conquered Egypt and the whole Near East. When he died (in his early thirties) his empire was divided up among his generals, but his dream of spreading Greek culture far and wide had begun to come true. This would help the spread of Christianity later on, but meanwhile it placed Judaism in serious danger.

At first, Judah was under the control of the new rulers of Egypt. These people, the Ptolemies, lived on friendly terms with God's people (now called JEWS, since most of them belonged to the tribe of Judah). In fact, many Jews went to live in Alexandria, Egypt, and a Greek translation of the Hebrew (G) Old Testament was made there for those Jews who spoke Greek. (This translation, called the Septuagint, would later be used by the early Church.)

In 196 B.C., Judah was taken over by the Seleucids, who ruled Syria. A few years later, trouble began. Some of the Jewish leaders decided that they wanted to be like the Gentiles (G) of the surrounding nations. The Seleucid king, Antiochus IV, was delighted. And a great persecution began. Antiochus tried to force **all** the Jews to be like the pagans in **all** things—including loose moral (G) standards and the worship of pagan gods.

All the precious vessels were taken from the temple of the Lord, and a statue (or altar—historians are not sure which) in honor of the pagan god Zeus was set up on top of the temple's altar of sacrifice.

Sacrifices to Yahweh were forbidden. Sacrifices to the pagan gods were commanded. When books of the Scriptures (G) were found, they were burned. Those who disobeyed the king's orders were punished by death. And many people **did** die rather than give in.

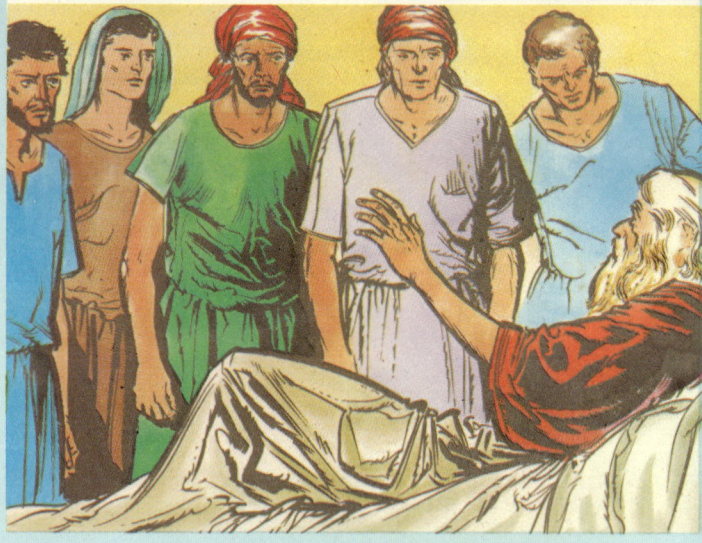

One of the many martyrs (G) of this period was ELEAZAR. Pagans or paganized Jews commanded him to eat food that the Jewish religion called "unclean" (not to be eaten). The reasons why God had told His people not to eat certain foods are hidden back in the dim history of the chosen people's beginnings. But this was part of the law that God's people were to follow until Jesus instituted the new law.

Eleazar, an old man of ninety, refused to eat the forbidden food. Those who tried to force him were old friends of his, probably fellow Jews who had become pagans. Because of this, they told him to eat **other** meat, which was "clean" for the Jews, and simply **pretend** to be eating forbidden meat.

Wouldn't that have been all right? No. It would have been like telling a lie—a lie in actions. And, as Eleazar himself said, he would also have given bad example, which could have caused other men to sin, too. "Even if I were to avoid the punishments of men," he declared, "I will never escape the punishment of God."

So Eleazar died a painful death, the death of a heroic martyr. Many other men, women and children did the same, including the mother of seven sons, who watched her boys being killed one by one and then suffered martyrdom herself.

Meanwhile, other faithful Jews had fled into the caves in the hills throughout Judah. There they lived on whatever they could find growing in the desert and on the mountains. Many of these people, too, were hunted down and massacred. And it was then that a group of their countrymen resolved to fight back.

The little band of fighting men, which grew rapidly as word spread, was led by a priest named Mattathias. His followers included his five sons: John, Simon, Judas, Eleazar and Jonathan.

These men went about tearing down pagan altars and driving their paganized countrymen out of the land.

Mattathias, however, was old and dying. So he gathered his sons about him and made Judas, who was called MACCABEUS, the general of their army.

As in the time of Joshua and the judges, God's people went out into battle and won victory after victory. After temporarily clearing most of the enemy troops out of the land, Judas and his men went up to Jerusalem. They wept to see the condition of the temple, with its gates partly burned and its courts full of weeds. Then they removed everything that the pagans had brought in, repaired the building and built a new altar. They held a great ceremony to re-dedicate the temple to Yahweh. Every year around the time of Christmas, the Jewish feast of HANUKKAH recalls this celebration.

Judas Maccabeus eventually died in battle, but his brothers Jonathan and Simon carried on after him until Judah was relatively free. Jonathan became high priest, and with Simon's son, John, the Hasmonean dynasty of kings began. But this dynasty did not last long. In 63 B.C. a Roman general, Pompey, conquered Jerusalem. Later, the Romans recognized a man named Herod as king. He is known to us as Herod the Great, who tried to have the Infant Jesus killed.

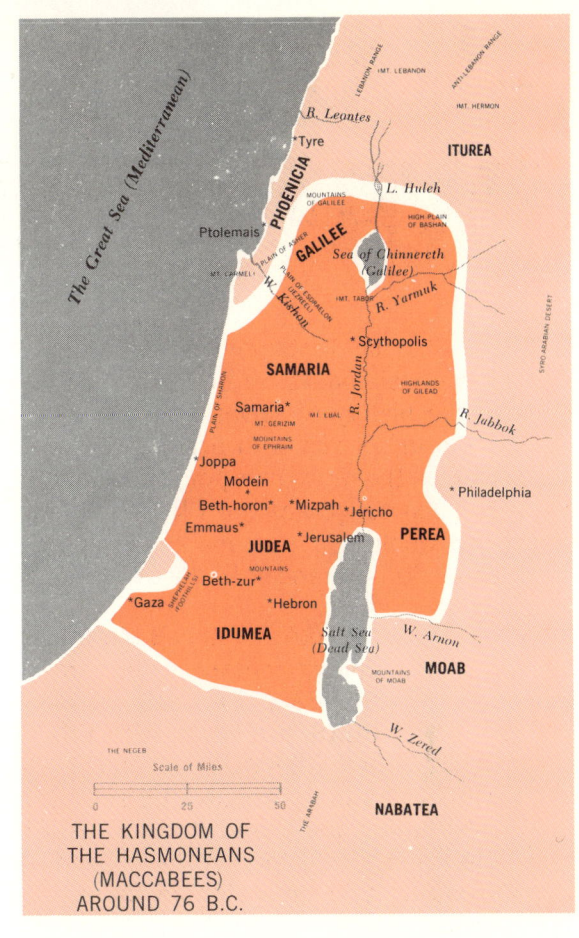

THE KINGDOM OF THE HASMONEANS (MACCABEES) AROUND 76 B.C.

Suggested Readings: Isaiah 55:3-13; Nehemiah 8:1-3, 5-6, 8, 18; 2 Maccabees 6:18-31; 1 Maccabees 3:3-9

What brought about the return of the exiles?
Because the exiles were sorry for their sins and the sins of their people, God inspired the Persian conqueror, Cyrus, to let them return to their homeland.

How did the Maccabean persecution come about?
King Antiochus wanted to spread Greek culture—including religion—throughout the Near East. Some of the chosen people were in favor of this, but many refused to be paganized. This situation led to the persecution.

Who can ascend the mountain of the Lord?
 or who may stand in his holy place?
He whose hands are sinless, whose heart is clean,
 who desires not what is vain,
 nor swears deceitfully to his neighbor.
He shall receive a blessing from the Lord,
 a reward from God his savior.
Such is the race that seeks for him,
 that seeks the face of the God of Jacob.

(Psalm 24:3-6)*

11 OTHER BIBLICAL "WHATS" AND "WHYS"

The Old Testament is made up of forty-six books. In our study of the history of salvation, we have come in contact with about twenty-four of them. At this point it would be good to look at the Old Testament as a whole and also see something about its references to Jesus.

The books of the Bible that chiefly contain **history** are GENESIS, EXODUS, NUMBERS, JOSHUA, JUDGES, RUTH, 1 and 2 SAMUEL, 1 and 2 KINGS, 1 and 2 CHRONICLES, EZRA, NEHEMIAH and 1 and 2 MACCABEES. The salvation history we have been studying is found mainly in these books.

The Book of LEVITICUS is grouped with the histories, but it chiefly contains laws regarding worship.

The Book of DEUTERONOMY, also grouped with the histories, urges faithfulness to the laws God gave through Moses.

Three other books grouped with the histories are TOBIT, ESTHER and JUDITH. Each of these books tells a story that has a worthwhile lesson for people of all times. Are they true stories? Not necessarily. But they **teach truths**—just as the parable of the good Samaritan teaches a truth.

Another group of Old Testament books is the collection called **the prophets.** We know about some of these prophets already, namely: ISAIAH (and "Second Isaiah"), JEREMIAH, EZEKIEL, HOSEA, AMOS, MICAH, HAGGAI and ZECHARIAH. These are the others:

NAHUM—who rejoiced over the fall of the cruel Assyrian Empire, which took place in 612 B.C.

HABAKKUK—who prophesied shortly after Nahum, warning that Yahweh would permit Babylon to punish Judah. But the prophet also promised:

The just man, because of his
    faith, shall live.
             (Habakkuk 2:4)*

ZEPHANIAH—who also prophesied shortly before the Exile, warning of punishment for unfaithfulness to Yahweh through sin.

OBADIAH—who wrote around the fifth century B.C., condemning the nation of Edom for fighting against Judah.

JOEL—who called the people to repentance and prayer around the middle of the fifth century B.C.

MALACHI—who also prophesied around the fifth century B.C. to urge that worship be carried out with mind and heart, not simply outwardly.

The book of JONAH is different from these other prophetical books. It is like a parable (a story with a lesson). God asks Jonah to preach in Nineveh, the Assyrian capital, to convert the Ninevites from their sins. Jonah is unwilling to go (in fact, he even tries to run away), because he doesn't want the Ninevites to be converted and forgiven by God. Who has the last word? God does. This book of the Bible shows that while God chose a certain people at one time in history, it was (and is) His plan to save all mankind.

The book of DANIEL is also different from the other prophetical books. It contains stories about an Israelite prophet named Daniel, living in Babylon during the Exile. But the book was written at the time of the Maccabees, and the stories were intended to encourage the Jewish people during Antiochus' persecution. Experts think that the author of the Book of Daniel wrote down stories that were already familiar to the Jews and added details that fitted the struggle his people had to go through around 165 B.C. The book of Daniel also contains chapters that are called **apocalyptic**—meaning that they give a message about a great struggle

SALVATION HISTORY IN THE OLD AND NEW TESTAMENTS

IMPORTANT STAGES IN SALVATION HISTORY	SOME IMPORTANT PEOPLE OF THESE TIMES	BOOKS WHICH TELL ABOUT THESE TIMES
(the centuries of pre-history)	our first parents	Genesis 1-11
God chooses a family from which His people will come (the time of the patriarchs—about 1850–1250 B.C.)	Abraham, Isaac, Jacob, Joseph and his brothers	Genesis 12-50, Exodus 1
The family becomes a united people (the Exodus and Sinai covenant—about 1250 to 1200)	Moses, Joshua	Exodus 2-40, Numbers, Deuteronomy
The people becomes a nation (the time of Joshua and the judges—about 1200 to 1020)	Joshua, Deborah, Gideon, Samson, Ruth, Samuel	Joshua, Judges, Ruth
The nation becomes a kingdom (the time of the first three kings—about 1020 to 932)	Samuel, Saul, David, Jonathan, Nathan, Solomon	1 and 2 Samuel, 1 Kings 1-10, 1 Chronicles 10-29, 2 Chronicles 1-9
The kingdom divides itself (the time of the two kingdoms—Israel and Judah—from 932 to 721)	Elijah, Elisha, Amos, Hosea, Isaiah, Micah	1 Kings 11-22, 2 Kings 1-17, 2 Chronicles 10-28, Amos, Hosea, Isaiah 1-39, Micah
Judah stands alone (the time between the Assyrian and Babylonian conquests—from 721 to 587)	Isaiah, Hezekiah, Josiah, Jeremiah	2 Kings 18-25, 2 Chronicles 29-36, Zephaniah, Jeremiah, Nahum, Habakkuk
Judah returns to its God (the time of the Babylonian Exile—587 to 538)	Ezekiel, "Second Isaiah"	Lamentations, Ezekiel, Isaiah 40-55
Judah returns to its homeland (the time of the Restoration and beginnings of Judaism—538 to 333)	Haggai, Zechariah, Ezra, Nehemiah	Haggai, Zechariah, Ezra, Nehemiah, Obadiah, Joel, Malachi
Judah shows its faithfulness (the time of the Seleucids, who gradually tried to paganize the Jews but eventually lost control of Palestine—333 to 63)	Judas Maccabeus and his brothers, Jonathan and Simon	1 and 2 Maccabees
The time of waiting draws to a close (the first years of the Jewish people under the Romans—63 to about 6 B.C.)	Mary and Joseph	(none)
God lives among men (the time from Jesus' incarnation to His ascension)	Jesus, Mary, Joseph, John the Baptizer, Peter, John....	Matthew, Mark, Luke, John
God sends His new people forth (the first years of the Church)	Mary, Peter, John, Paul, Luke....	Acts of the Apostles, Galatians, 1 and 2 Corinthians, 2 Timothy and other epistles

between good and evil, written in symbolic form, where almost everything stands for something else. Again, the purpose of these chapters seems to be to encourage the persecuted.

The other books listed among the prophets are LAMENTATIONS, (five poems of sorrow over the destruction of Jerusalem) and BARUCH, a book of instruction and encouragement that was probably written after the return from the Exile.

The remaining seven books of the Old Testament are called **wisdom** books. Written in the style of Hebrew poetry, most of them have the purpose of teaching us about ourselves, our life on earth, and our relationship with God. But they do not give us all the answers, since God's revelation to men would reach its high point only with Jesus Christ.

The first wisdom book in the Bible is JOB, which looks into (but does not solve) the problem of suffering in life.

The Book of PSALMS gives us 150 beautiful prayer-songs. There are several types, such as: hymns of praise, songs of sorrow, songs of trust in God, songs of thanksgiving, songs about the Davidic king, songs about Jerusalem, songs with a teaching purpose.

The Book of PROVERBS is a collection of wise sayings, such as:

Walk with wise men and you will
  become wise,
 but the companion of fools will
  fare badly.
(Proverbs 13:20)*

ECCLESIASTES, or QOHELETH, treats the passing nature of life (without speaking of the life to come).

The SONG OF SONGS is a love poem, which many people think is a parable showing God's love for His people.

The Book of WISDOM seems to have been written to show that true wisdom comes from God and not from Greek philosophers (who were very popular at the time). This book, together with Daniel and 2 Maccabees, speaks of reward or punishment in the future life. Earlier books of the Bible don't mention this. (Daniel and 2 Maccabees even speak of the resurrection of the dead.)

The Book of SIRACH, or ECCLESIASTICUS, helps us to think more deeply about God's law and the importance of keeping it.

We have already mentioned that some persons, places and events of the Old Testament may be thought of as looking forward to (foreshadowing) **later** persons, places and events. We mentioned this, for example, with regard to the Passover and paschal lamb (Jesus' sacrifice) and the manna in the desert (the Eucharist). When we think of persons, places or events in this way, we call them **types.**

Some Old Testament personalities may even be thought of as types of Jesus. Two of these are Moses and David.

Moses was a mediator (G) between God and His people. He spoke for God to the people, and he prayed to Him for them. This is what a mediator does. Jesus did the same during His life on earth. And He continues to do so even now. He speaks His Father's words to us through the Gospels and He offers the Mass—the greatest prayer—to the Father for us. The Israelites thought of Moses as their "savior" or "liberator," although, of course, it was really Yahweh who set them free. Jesus is our true Liberator—the Savior of the world—who died and rose to make up for our sins and give us the chance to share His everlasting joy in heaven.

David was the king of God's people, who received the promise of an everlasting dynasty. Now Jesus is the King of God's people, and His kingship will never end.

Besides the Old Testament passages that contain types, certain other passages, too, contain a deeper meaning. For example, there are other references to Jesus, although not by name.

We find passages like this in such wisdom books as the Psalms and Wisdom, in such historical books as Deuteronomy and 2 Samuel, and especially in some of the books of the prophets. Sometimes when a prophet was speaking to the people of his time and place about their own situation, God would also intend the words to refer to the MESSIAH—the Anointed One, descended from David, who would establish Yahweh's lasting kingdom in the world. We know this because the Messiah Himself (Jesus) and His early followers have pointed out some of these passages.

The prophets foretold (more or less clearly) that the Messiah would be a king, descended from David, born of a virgin, born in Bethlehem, a suffering servant of

God, the ruler of the world. They also foretold that He would make a NEW COVENANT between God and man:

> The days are coming, says the Lord, when I will make a new covenant with the house of Israel and the house of Judah. It will not be like the covenant I made with their fathers the day I took them by the hand to lead them forth from the land of Egypt; for they broke my covenant and I had to show myself their master, says the Lord. But this is the covenant which I will make with the house of Israel after those days, says the Lord. I will place my law within them, and write it upon their hearts; I will be their God, and they shall be my people.
> (Jeremiah 31:31-33)*

This covenant was to last forever. As we know, the new covenant was sealed in the blood of Christ.

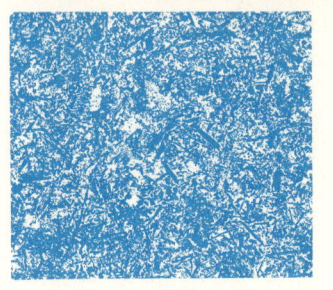

Suggested Readings: Isaiah 7:14; 9:1-6; 11:1-9; Micah 5:1; Jeremiah 23:1-6; Zechariah 9:9-10; Isaiah 53:3-6; Daniel 7:13-14

How may the Old Testament be divided?
We may divide the Old Testament into historical books, prophetical books and wisdom books.

What is a "type"?
A type is a person, place or thing written about in the Bible which was intended by God to foreshadow a future person, place or thing.

Where does the Old Testament especially speak of Jesus?
The Old Testament especially speaks of Jesus in some of the books of the prophets.

> God, give your own justice to the king,
>   your own righteousness to the royal son,
> so that he may rule your people rightly
>   and your poor with justice.
> Let the mountains and hills
>   bring a message of peace for the people.
> Uprightly he will defend the poorest,
> he will save the children of those in need,
>   and crush their oppressors.
> Like sun and moon he will endure,
>   age after age,
> welcome as rain that falls on the pasture,
>   and showers to thirsty soil.
> (Psalm 72:1-6)**

12
THE MYSTERY OF JESUS

Unit 3
He Comes To Live Among Us

Elizabeth was happy. For so many years she had hoped and prayed that she and Zechariah would have a child. Now, at last, her dream was coming true! As she went about her household duties, she thanked Yahweh again and again for the wonderful gift He was giving them.

Perhaps she paused from time to time to gaze out at the Judean mountains, which had witnessed God's saving deeds down through the centuries. Another saving deed was about to take place, for it had been revealed to her husband Zechariah that this child—this son of theirs who would soon be born—was to have a special mission from God. Was the long-awaited Messiah coming? Would their child be a prophet to prepare the way for him?

Many of the Jewish people **did** think that the messianic age was about to begin. Many thought that the Messiah, the Son of David, would free Palestine (G) from the Romans and rule over the Jewish people as king in God's name. The deeply religious people of Qumran also seemed to be expecting great leaders. At any rate, it was a wonderful age to be living in, a time of hope and promise.

On that particular day in or around the year 6 B.C., a graceful young woman suddenly appeared at the doorway of Elizabeth's home.

"Peace be to you, Elizabeth!"
MARY OF NAZARETH stepped into the shadowy room to embrace her aging kinswoman. Suddenly Elizabeth knew that the Mother of the Messiah was standing right here before her!

Joyful over what God had just revealed to her, she exclaimed:

"Of all women you are the most blessed, and blessed is the fruit of your womb. Why should I be honored with a visit from the mother of my Lord? For the moment your greeting reached my ears, the child in my womb leapt for joy. Yes, blessed is she who believed that the promise made her by the Lord would be fulfilled."

(Luke 1:42-45)**

55

Mary had believed in a promise from God—that by His power (and **only** by His power) she was to become the Mother of a child who would be called Son of the Most High, a child to whom God would give the throne of David His father. She had believed and had given her consent:

"I am the servant of the Lord. Let it be done to me as you say."
(Luke 1:38)*

Did she know that this "Yes" of hers was to change the course of history? Perhaps not, but seeing that Elizabeth now knew her secret, Mary broke into a hymn of praise to God, who had done such great things for her and for His people. Mary was grateful and humble; she loved God deeply. For these very reasons He had chosen her to be the Mother of the Messiah.

A few months after the birth of Elizabeth's son, John, the Romans announced that everyone in Palestine had to return to his family town to register in a census. This took place around the year 6 B.C.

Why "B.C."? According to our way of thinking, this should have been the year 1 A.D.! The explanation is simple. When Christians of the sixth century A.D. decided that the calendar should be dated from Christ's birth, they tried to figure out when it had taken place—how many years before their

"Bethlehem...from you shall come forth...one who is to be ruler"
—Micah 5:1*

current year. And not having as much historical information as we have today, they made a mistake of about six years.

JOSEPH, a descendant of David, set out for Bethlehem, David's birthplace. He took Mary with him in order to look after her, since the child was to be born any day now.

We know the rest. Every place where travelers could have stayed was filled, because so many people had returned to Bethlehem. The weary couple had to be content with a cave where animals were kept. And there JESUS was born.

Why in a cold, clammy cave with prickly straw for a mattress? Because — as we could see if we were to read the New Testament carefully — this was Jesus' way of doing things. Real love goes through hardships for the person(s) loved. Jesus gave His very all from the very beginning of His life to show His love for us.

Perhaps He was born during a cold season as well. Fourth-century Christians chose December 25 as the date for celebrating Christmas, in order to counteract a pagan festival held in honor of the sun. These Christians didn't know the **real** date of Jesus' birth. Neither do we.

God had made known to Joseph the name by which the child was to be called. "Jesus" is a Greek form of Joshua, a name that originally meant "Yahweh helps." By Jesus' time it had taken on the meaning "Yahweh saves."

What a perfect name! Later on, Jesus would reveal the fact that He is GOD and that He had come to lay down His very life to SAVE us.

Later, people also called Jesus "Christ." In fact, St. Paul did so often. CHRIST is another word for Messiah, so to say "Jesus Christ" is the same as saying Jesus the Messiah.

We find that each of the four GOSPELS treats the early life of Jesus differently.

The Gospel of ST. MARK follows the order of events that St. Peter preached about in the early years of the Church. St. Peter concentrated on Jesus' miracles, teachings, death and resurrection — events he himself had seen and heard. Since Peter didn't speak about the events of Jesus' infancy, Mark didn't write about them at all.

The Gospel of ST. MATTHEW concentrates on Jesus as the Messiah, who fulfilled various passages of the Old Testament and was descended from David through His legal father, Joseph. (**Legal** descent meant much more to the Jewish people of Jesus' time than it does to us today.) So Matthew gives much importance to Old Testament quotations and to the role of St. Joseph.

When speaking about Jesus' birth and infancy, the Gospel of ST. LUKE emphasizes Mary, rather than Joseph, as Matthew does. In the first two chapters of his Gospel, Luke already mentions certain themes that are favorites with him, such as the Holy Spirit's activity, Christian joy, the poor who love God, prayer....

ST. JOHN's Gospel begins with a beautiful hymn — perhaps one that Christians were already using in worship. This hymn stresses the fact that Jesus is God, which is one of the main themes of John's whole Gospel.

Just from this quick summary, we can see that the four Gospels — the books of the Bible that tell us about Jesus' life and teachings — are somewhat different from one another. We will soon see more about this. The four Gospels **complete** one another. Together they give us a marvelous picture of the most perfect man who ever lived — Jesus.

The young Jesus was a mystery to His Mother and foster father. Even though He had come to them in a completely miraculous way, He seemed like such an ordinary boy! He asked questions and learned the answers. He grew taller and stronger. He was full of energy and enthusiastically helped Mary and Joseph with their daily work. He was kind, thoughtful and obedient.

Jesus is a mystery to us, too, even though the Church, guided by the Holy Spirit, has been able to tell us much about Him. What we **do** know for certain is this: Jesus is one Person, the Second Person of the Blessed Trinity. So Jesus is God. But this one Person has two natures—the nature of GOD and the nature of MAN (human nature like ours, except that, being God, He could never sin). This fact is a MYSTERY of our Faith, which means a great truth revealed by God which we will never be able to fully understand.

Therefore, the mystery of Jesus **remains** a mystery for us. It may have been even less clear for Joseph (and even Mary) in those early years.

St. Luke has given us one precious story from Jesus' childhood. It was spring, probably in the year 8 A.D. Twelve-year-old Jesus had gone to Jerusalem with Mary and Joseph for the celebration of the Passover, that great feast in which the Jewish people recalled their liberation from Egypt by Yahweh through Moses.

The celebration lasted eight days, but Luke does not tell us whether the Holy Family stayed for the entire feast. At any rate, Mary and Joseph set out for Nazareth with a caravan, each of them thinking that Jesus, too, was somewhere in the long, straggling procession of people and animals. But even though they were sure He must be in the caravan, they began to look for Him among their relatives and friends.

The caravan stopped for the night. No Jesus. Maybe He had left Jerusalem later, walking with a group that would join them during the night....

Morning came. Still no Jesus. Mary and Joseph started back toward Jerusalem.

And it was there in Jerusalem that they found Him, in one of the outer halls of the temple, seated among the rabbis who usually taught there daily, listening to them intently and answering the questions that they, in their turn, put to this bright, young lad.

The worried couple came forward until Jesus saw and greeted them. Mary spoke first, and her words showed the anxiety she had suffered:

"Son, why have you done this to us? See how worried your father and I have been, looking for you."

Jesus' gentle answer really surprised them. For He said, "Why were you looking for me? Didn't you realize that I had to be in my Father's house, about His business?"

His Father! Until then He had never called anyone His Father but Joseph. Could He be speaking of God? But who had ever been heard to call God "Father"?

Suggested Readings: Matthew 1:18—2:23; Luke 1:5—2:52; John 1:1-5, 14

What are the Gospels?
The Gospels of Matthew, Mark, Luke and John are the four books of the New Testament that give us the life and teachings of Jesus.

How is Jesus both God and man?
Jesus is one Person, and that Person is divine (God). But He has two natures—the nature of God and the nature of a human being. This is a mystery of our Faith.

What does the name Jesus Christ mean?
Jesus means "God saves." Christ means the "Messiah," the one who was to establish God's lasting kingdom.

"Blessed be the Lord, the God of Israel,
for he has visited his people, he has come to their rescue
and he has raised up for us a power for salvation
in the House of his servant David,
even as he proclaimed,
by the mouth of his holy prophets from ancient times,
that he would save us from our enemies
and from the hands of all who hate us.
Thus he shows mercy to our ancestors,
thus he remembers his holy covenant,
the oath he swore
to our father Abraham
that he would grant us, free from fear,
to be delivered from the hands of our enemies,
to serve him in holiness and virtue
in his presence, all our days."

(Luke 1:68-75)

13 ECHOES OF THE EXODUS

The crowds pressed close, trying to hear the fiery preacher and catch a glimpse of him. From Jerusalem and all Judea, from Perea and even from the shores of Galilee, they had come to listen to JOHN's words and receive his baptism of repentance.

Those who craned their necks or pushed their way closer saw a man in his early or mid-thirties, his face bronzed from years of exposure to the desert sun, his garment the simple, hairy camel skin of a prophet.

Those who strained their ears to listen heard such warnings as:

"Every tree that is not fruitful will be cut down and thrown into the fire."

(Matthew 3:10)*

"The one who will follow me is more powerful than I. I am not even fit to carry his sandals.... His winnowing-fan is in his hand. He will clear the threshing floor and gather his grain into the barn, but the chaff he will burn in unquenchable fire."

(Matthew 3:11-12)*

Most of the people got the message. It would be far better to be sorry for sin and turn over a new leaf than to face the punishment of the "one" who was coming.

As others had already done during these last few months, the people lined up to show their repentance (G) by being baptized. It was a symbolic washing that indicated their good intentions—nothing more than that. But we human beings **need** to express ourselves with symbols and signs.

John baptized them one by one in the waters of the Jordan, which were not too cold even though it was winter. As the day drew to a close, they began to depart for their cities, towns and farms, leaving the Baptizer with his enthusiastic group of disciples (G)— men who had taken advantage of the slack season of the year to stay with the new prophet and learn more about his teachings.

One day during that winter (probably of 27-28 A.D.) John the Baptizer said to his disciples, "Look.... There is the one whom I said is to come after me, the one who is greater than I because He was before me."

The disciples looked in the direction John had indicated and saw a man about the same age as the Baptizer walking by. John continued, "I have to admit that at first I didn't recognize Him, even though the very reason that I came baptizing with water was so that He might be made known to Israel. I saw the Spirit come down from the sky like a dove, and it came to rest on Him."

The Baptizer was recalling Jesus' baptism, which had taken place just recently. John couldn't understand why someone so holy (G) had come to receive the baptism of repentance. But for some reason Jesus had wanted it that way. He had begun His mission by passing through the waters of the Jordan, just as the nation of Israel had begun **its** mission by passing through the waters of the Reed Sea.

John's disciples were fascinated. Who could this man be? The Messiah?

The next day, when the Baptizer pointed Jesus out again, two disciples realized what they should do. Giving John a grateful glance, they set out after this new leader.

Jesus turned and saw them. "What are you looking for?" He asked.

"Rabbi," they replied, "Where do You live?"

"Come and see."

They did, and they stayed. Later, one of them, whose name was Andrew, went to call his brother Simon. "We have found the Messiah!" Andrew exclaimed. Then he brought Simon to Jesus, who said, "You are Simon son of John. You will be called Kepha." Kepha meant "rock" in Aramaic, the ordinary language of the Jewish people at the time of Jesus. We know the name better in its English form, which comes from a Greek translation: PETER.

The next months were exciting ones for Peter and his friends. The group of Jesus' followers began to grow, and what things they saw!

At a wedding in the town of Cana, to which all of them had been invited, they heard Jesus' Mother tell Him that the wine had run out. The next thing they knew, six stone jars that had held water were suddenly full of delicious red wine!

When Jesus was teaching at a Sabbath service in the synagogue of Capernaum, a man possessed by the devil began to scream at Him. "Be quiet!" exclaimed Jesus. "Come out of him!" Suddenly the man underwent a convulsion and became as gentle as a lamb.

Peter invited Jesus to visit his home, where his mother-in-law was very sick with a fever. When Jesus was brought to her, He took her by the hand and helped her to get up. The fever left her at once.

Good news of this sort travels fast, and soon people from all over Capernaum were bringing their sick to Jesus, who cured them all. What enthusiasm there was for this new prophet!

Then He escaped to a lonely place outside the town to pray. When His disciples found Him, He told them, "Let's move on to the neighboring villages, so that I may preach there, too. This is why I have come."

In the Gospel of St. Matthew, we find that the evangelist (Gospel writer) likes to compare Jesus with Moses. It is easy to see why, when we know that Matthew was chiefly writing for people who knew the Old Testament. Since his audience regarded the giving of the law on Mount Sinai as one of the high points in Israel's history, the evangelist collected those teachings of Jesus that made the law more perfect. And he presented them in a famous section of his Gospel called the SERMON ON THE MOUNT. Anyone who studies this sermon and tries to understand it will see that a true follower of Jesus is a real hero.

The sermon begins with the eight BEATITUDES—promises of happiness in heaven (and maybe sometimes even on earth) for those who want to grow closer to God, who put Him first in their lives, who are sorry to see Him offended, who are gentle and humble, who want to be like Jesus, who forgive and forget, who are free from attachments to sin, who make peace, who are ready to go through sufferings because of their loyalty to God.

The spirit of the beatitudes is a spirit of love for God and others.

Who lived the beatitudes most perfectly? Jesus Himself. He lived for His Father and for people—spending His nights in prayer, spending His days in teaching and healing. After Jesus comes Mary, His Mother. The Gospels say little about her, but in that little her great love for God and others shines out very clearly.

The spirit of the beatitudes is the spirit of "God's poor ones"—persons who hunger for Him, who cling to Him and let Him be the strength that they need in their weakness.

The sermon on the mount continues with advice to really **live** by Jesus' teachings so that other people will be drawn to God, too. And farther on Jesus explains that it's not enough to act as a good Christian **part** of the time. Our dedication to God must be **full-time**, not just for show.

Jesus also explains that He has come to make God's law more perfect, and He gives some examples regarding various COMMANDMENTS. The rich, full meaning of the commandments with which we are familiar was given to them by Jesus.

Jesus explains the importance of PRAYER and our need to trust in God without worrying uselessly. He warns us to be on our guard against people who seem to be His followers but really aren't. We mustn't let them lead us away from Him.

The sermon on the mount also contains a famous quotation and a famous prayer.

The quotation is:

"Treat others the way that you would have them treat you."
(Matthew 7:12)*

The prayer is the OUR FATHER, which the Gospels have given us in two versions. One of the most amazing facts that Jesus revealed to us is that Yahweh, the living God, permits us to call Him "Father"!

Jesus ends the sermon on the mount with some words of warning:

"Anyone who hears my words and puts them into practice is like the wise man who built his house on rock. When the rainy season set in, the torrents came and the winds blew and buffeted his house. It did not collapse; it had been solidly set on rock. Anyone who hears my words but does not put them into practice is like the foolish man who built his house on sandy ground. The rains fell, the torrents came, the winds blew and lashed against his house. It collapsed under all this and was completely ruined."
(Matthew 7:24-27)*

Suggested Readings: Matthew 3:1-17; John 1:29-42; 2:1-11; Mark 1:23-39; Matthew 5:1—7:29

What is the sermon on the mount?
The sermon on the mount is a famous collection of some of Jesus' most important teachings, including the beatitudes.

What is the spirit of the beatitudes?
The spirit of the beatitudes is the spirit of "God's poor ones," who love and rely on God and love everyone else as well.

Who lived the beatitudes most perfectly?
The beatitudes were lived most perfectly by Jesus and His Mother, Mary.

"Father, may your name be held holy,
your kingdom come;
give us each day our daily bread,
and forgive us our sins,
for we ourselves forgive each one who is in debt to us.
And do not put us to the test."
(Luke 11:2-4)**

14 BREAD FOR GOD'S PEOPLE

Storm winds buffeted the little boat, and angry waves threatened to swamp it. Yet Jesus slept on. He had spent the day preaching to the crowds on the shore, and doubtless He had passed a few recent nights in prayer, as was His custom. Now no raging sea could bother Him, even though the waves were crashing against the boat's hull.

As fishermen, several of the disciples were used to those savage storms that often spring up on the Sea of Galilee. But that fact didn't make the situation any less frightening. They were far from land; how could all of them survive if their small craft were overturned? When at last they couldn't stand it any longer, they woke Jesus.

He sat up and took in the situation. "Quiet!" He said. "Be still!" At once the wind fell off and the waves subsided. In a few moments the sea was calm.

"Who is He?" the disciples asked one another. Never had they seen the likes of this—just as they had never before seen anyone bring a dead boy back to life, as Jesus had done recently in the town of Naim.

What would He do next?

Jesus was popular at this point in His public life (G)—popular as a healer, popular as a teacher. Great crowds followed Him as He moved about Galilee.

One particular spring day, He worked a miracle that is retold in all four Gospels because of its importance.

That day Jesus was trying to avoid the crowds and spend some time alone with His apostles. He decided to use the lake (the Sea of Galilee) as an escape route. But the crowds were hungry for His words and began to walk along the shore....

Jesus and His apostles disembarked at a lonely spot and set off up a hillside. Then they saw the people coming, and Jesus felt pity for them because "they were like sheep without a shepherd."

He began to cure their sick. After that, He taught them there on the hillside until it grew quite late.

"Teacher," said the apostles, "maybe You should send the people away so they can go into the farms and villages and buy themselves something to eat."

"There's no need to send them away," replied Jesus. "You yourselves give them some food.... Philip, where shall we buy bread for these people to eat?"

"Even two hundred days' wages would only buy enough bread to give each of them a small piece," Philip answered. The crowd really was enormous from the viewpoint of eating!

"How many loaves do you have?" Jesus persisted.

"There's a boy here who has five loaves of bread and two dried fish," replied Andrew. "But what good is that among so many?"

"Have the people sit down," said Jesus. He took the five loaves and two fish and gave them to His disciples to distribute. They started to do so, and kept on until everyone had enough to eat.

"Gather up everything that's left over," Jesus directed, "so nothing will be wasted." They collected twelve large baskets of scraps.

"This must be the prophet who is to come into the world!" said someone. The idea caught on, and word spread. Jesus saw what was likely to happen. A few minutes more and they would be making Him king! Imagine what the results of **that** would be, with Rome ruling Palestine! Jesus would be expected to lead a rebellion against Rome—Jesus, whom the prophet Isaiah had described as "Prince of Peace"—Jesus, whose kingdom was one of the spirit only.

"Get into the boat and go back across the lake," He told the apostles. Meanwhile, He slipped away and lost Himself in the hills.

Yes, Jesus was at the height of His popularity. Wherever He went, people would scurry off to get their sick. They laid them on bedrolls in the marketplaces of the towns through which He passed, and all who touched even the tassel of His cloak got well.

But there was something wrong with the enthusiasm of these people, and Jesus was fully aware of it. To those who came swarming after Him the day after He had multiplied the loaves, He said, "You're looking for me because you had all the bread you wanted."

Yes, that was it. So Jesus reminded them, "Work for food that lasts to eternal life, the kind of food that the Son of Man will give you.... Believe in the one whom God has sent."

"Give us a sign so we'll see that we should believe in you," they asked. "Our fathers had manna in the desert. The Scriptures say, 'He gave them bread from heaven to eat.'"

"I am the bread of life," Jesus told them. "Those who come to me will never be hungry. Those who believe in me will never thirst.... I am the living bread that has come down from heaven."

Was Jesus speaking of His **teachings**? Perhaps He was, for God's Word has often been called spiritual bread. But then our Savior continued with some of the most amazing expressions found in all of the Gospels, and here the bread He spoke of was clearly something else:

"Anyone who eats this bread will
 live for ever;
and the bread that I shall give
is my flesh, for the life of the world....
If you do not eat the flesh of the
 Son of Man
and drink his blood,
you will not have life in you.
Anyone who does eat my flesh and
 drink my blood
has eternal life,
and I shall raise him up on the last
 day.
For my flesh is real food
and my blood is real drink."
(John 6:51-55)**

And there it was—Jesus' mysterious promise of the EUCHARIST, by which we, His followers, become one with Him, growing in that life of His which we must share in order to enter everlasting life in heaven. Through the Eucharist and the other sacraments, we receive the effects of Jesus' passion and death. In other words, through the Eucharist and the other sacraments Jesus **saves** us.

It was probably about a year before the Last Supper that our Savior promised this wonderful gift of His very self. How eager He must have been to give us this gift!

In the Eucharist our Savior draws us closer to Himself and makes us more like Him. He makes us holier by grace, a sharing in His own life. He draws us closer to all God's people in love and gives us spiritual light to know God's truths and spiritual energy to serve Him and others.

Only He could have thought of such a wonderful gift, which comes into our lives through the miracle that takes place daily at the Consecration of every Mass.

Each of the four GOSPELS tells us about the multiplication of the loaves, because the early Christians saw a close relationship between that miracle and the daily miracle of the Eucharist. But each evangelist (Gospel writer) has included different details. Why? For one thing, each of them had a different purpose in writing his Gospel. Also, they may well have used different sources of information. As with the books of the Old Testament, the Gospels weren't written down right

PALESTINE AT THE TIME OF JESUS

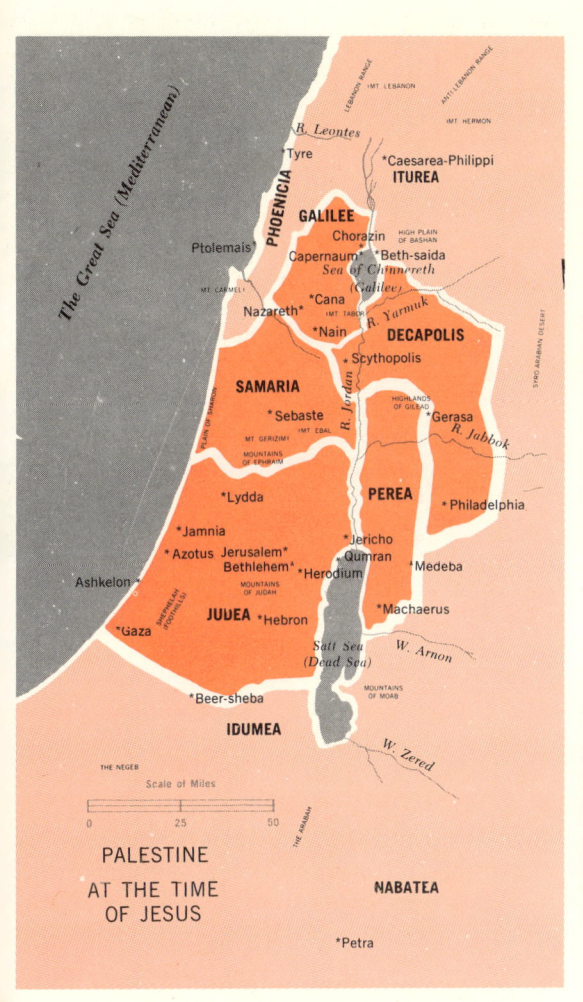

away. First they were passed on orally in the Christian community. The peoples of the ancient Near East had good memories. They would memorize and retell what various apostles preached. And we can imagine that no two apostles described an event of Jesus' life in exactly the same words. So this explains some of the differences among the Gospels.

Here are a few facts about the four Gospels:

They do not try to give us the **complete** life of Jesus, nor do they necessarily retell events in their real time-order.

The editions we have now were first written in Greek, probably between 60 and 100 A.D. (Mark first, John last).

Mark's is the shortest Gospel and probably was the first to be finished.

Matthew's Gospel seems to have gone through two distinct editions, the first one in Aramaic (the language of the Jews at that time) and a second—thoroughly rewritten—edition, which was done in Greek.

The Gospels of Matthew and Luke treat most of the events and teachings in the Gospel of Mark, but Matthew and Luke also give us other information about Jesus that had been passed on orally or even in writing.

John's Gospel usually does not repeat the events and teachings found in Matthew, Mark and Luke. Rather

The Plain of Esdraelon

The Desert of Judah

it gives us new information, together with reflections about the deeper meanings of events.

John's Gospel may have been largely written by his disciples, with him as their chief source of information.

The Church, guided by the Holy Spirit, declares that the Gospels tell us the honest truth about Jesus. And, indeed, they would have to! If a Gospel had contained anything untrue, the early Christians—who knew Jesus' teachings and the events of His life by heart—would have objected at once.

So we are sure about the accuracy of the Gospels, which, like the rest of the Bible, can truly be called the "bread of God's Word."

Suggested Readings: Mark 4:35-41; Matthew 14:13-21, 34-36; John 6:1-15; 26-58

Why is the miracle of the loaves considered especially important?
The miracle of the loaves is considered especially important because of its relationship to the Eucharist.

What is the Eucharist?
The Eucharist is the sacrament of Jesus' complete presence under the appearances of bread and wine.

Do the Gospels give us the complete life of Jesus?
The Gospels do not give us the complete life of Jesus, but only certain events and teachings that were passed on orally in the early Christian community.

Do the Gospels tell us the truth about Jesus?
The Gospels **do** tell us the truth about Jesus. We are especially sure because the Church (guided by the Holy Spirit) has told us so.

A lamp to my feet is your word,
a light to my path.
(Psalm 119:105)*

15 HIS CLOSEST FOLLOWERS

The Old Testament had its great men and women, such as Abraham, Joseph, Moses, Joshua, Deborah, Ruth, David, Isaiah, Jeremiah, Josiah and Judas Maccabeus. The Church, too, has had its great men and women —many saints in every century, who were heroes of God, shining lights for their fellowmen.

The central figure of the Bible and of history, of course, is JESUS. He was the only **perfect** man who ever lived.

Everyone on earth has good qualities, but no one has them **all**. And everyone also has bad qualities. For example, someone with a great intelligence may look down on others or may not lead a good life. Someone who has a strong determination and works hard to get ahead in the

Nazareth

Sea of Galilee

world may not be sympathetic and understanding toward others.

But Jesus was perfect—wise, humble, completely good, firmly determined to do His Father's will, brave, truthful, sympathetic....

The more we read the Gospels, the more ways of imitating Jesus we can see. He calls us to become as much like Him as possible, which is what the great saints did.

The greatest saint of all is Jesus' own Mother, MARY.
Because she had been chosen by God to be His Mother, Mary received special gifts and privileges from Him, such as coming into existence without original sin. We call this privilege the IMMACULATE CONCEPTION.

Throughout her life, Mary grew in GRACE (God's life) and in all the VIRTUES. A virtue is the power and habit of doing good. Some of the main virtues are faith (believing without seeing), hope (trust in God's help for reaching heaven), love for God and others (which includes keeping the ten commandments and serving others through good deeds, such as the works of mercy), prudence (keeping heaven in view when we plan our actions), justice (being fair to God and to everyone else), fortitude (having the courage to do what is right in spite of any difficulty) and temperance (self-control).

Helped by God's grace and His actual graces (G), Mary grew steadily in these seven virtues and in all the other virtues, too (such as humility and obedience). She had a great spirit of prayer, and loved to think about Jesus' teachings so as to put them into practice in her own life. She always used God's gifts and special help in the best way. This is why we admire Mary and try to imitate her. She was wholeheartedly **for God**.

The APOSTLES, too, became great heroes of God, but this didn't happen immediately. The Gospels often mention the apostles' shortcomings, and this gives us courage, for we see that **anyone** can become a saint if he or she is loyal to Jesus, prays for God's help and tries to live as God wants us to live.

We know that one of the apostles refused God's help at some point. Early in His public life, Jesus had chosen Peter, Andrew, James, John, Philip, Bartholomew, Matthew, Thomas, James, Jude Thaddeus, Simon and Judas. A few months later,

He declared, "Didn't I myself choose the twelve of you? Yet one of you is a devil." It seems that Judas Iscariot had already begun to reject the graces of God. How did Judas begin to fall? We don't know. But this should be a lesson for all of us. We can't remain close to God if we start to play around with sin instead of using the special help He is constantly giving us.

The apostle we know the most about is PETER, whom Jesus chose to be the leader of the Twelve. One of the most interesting Gospel stories about this apostle has as its setting the night after the multiplication of the loaves. Jesus had told the apostles to cross the lake again, while He went into the hills to pray.

A strong headwind was blowing. As the men were struggling to row against the waves, they saw something passing by them in the darkness. Or was it some**one**? A ghost? Someone **was** walking past them on the water!

"Courage!" called a voice. "It is I! Don't be afraid!"

At once Peter cried out, "Lord, if it's really You, tell me to come to You across the water!"

"Come."

So Peter stepped over the boat's gunwale and started to walk toward Jesus. Everything was fine until he realized what he was doing. Then Peter panicked, and as soon as he did, he began to sink. "Lord!" he wailed, "save me!" Instantly he felt Jesus' strong grip on him, and all was well again.

"How little faith you have," Jesus scolded gently. "Why did you doubt?"

The early Christians liked to tell this story because it symbolizes Jesus' nearness to the Church (the "boat of Peter"), even when the Church is in rough waters. It also shows the importance of faith.

After Jesus had explained how important it is to believe in Him and receive the Eucharist, many of His followers left Him. "Do you want to go away, too?" He asked the apostles.

As usual, Peter spoke for them all:

"Lord, who shall we go to? You have the message of eternal life, and we believe; we know that you are the Holy One of God."

(John 6:68-69)**

We find these words in John's Gospel. In Matthew's there is a similar declaration of faith by Peter. It took place in pagan territory

71

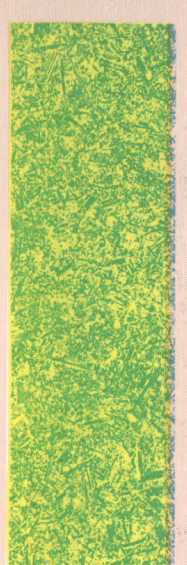

north of the Sea of Galilee, where Jesus was alone with His disciples.

"In the opinion of the people, who am I?" Jesus asked.

The disciples had various answers to give:

"Some say John the Baptizer."

"Some say Elijah."

"Some say Jeremiah or another prophet."

"And who do **you** say that I am?" Jesus continued.

"You are the Messiah," Simon Peter answered, "the Son of the living God!"

(Matthew 16:16)*

It was the answer that Jesus had wanted. Joyfully He replied:

"Blest are you, Simon, son of John! No mere man has revealed this to you, but my heavenly Father."

(Matthew 16:17)*

At this point St. Matthew adds a very important promise made by Jesus to Peter. Some scripture experts think that Jesus made this promise after His resurrection. (We remember that the Gospels don't necessarily tell us the events of our Savior's life in order.) But the promise is important because of **what it says,** not because of when it was made:

"I for my part declare to you, you are 'Rock,' and on this rock I will build my church, and the jaws of death shall not prevail against it. I will entrust to you the keys of the kingdom of heaven. Whatever you declare bound on earth shall be bound in heaven; whatever you declare loosed on earth shall be loosed in heaven."

(Matthew 16:18-19)*

How rich in meaning these words were! Jesus was saying that Peter ("the rock") would somehow be the foundation of the community of His followers; that this community (the Church) would not be overcome even by death; and that Peter was to be its leader. (Being keeper of the "keys" and having the power to call something "bound" or "loosed" meant having authority.)

What authority was Peter to have? As time went on, this would become clearer and clearer. Under the guidance of the Holy Spirit, the members of Jesus' CHURCH (the "kingdom" or "reign" of God) would recognize that the Church's chief leader had—and always **will** have—the power to teach them what to believe, how to live and how to grow in holiness.

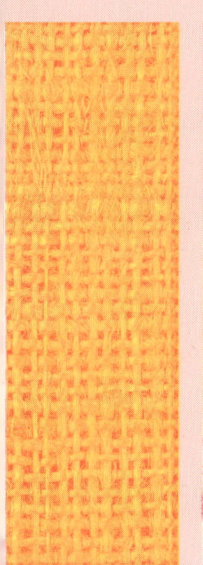

The Church's chief leader is called the POPE. Peter was the first Pope; the present Pope is his successor. In between these two there have been over two hundred other Popes. When a man becomes Pope, he acquires special help from the Holy Spirit so that any important declaration he makes about faith (what we should believe) or morals (what we should do) will be free from mistakes. This special privilege from God is called INFALLIBILITY. God has given this gift to the Pope (and to certain meetings of the bishops united with the Pope) in order that we may truly know what we must believe and do in order to reach heaven.

In the Gospel, Jesus speaks of His Church as the kingdom of heaven, the kingdom of God or the reign of God. All of these mean a community whose leader is God. Jesus is always the head of His Church. But because we cannot see Him, we call Him the **invisible** head of the Church. The Pope, who speaks for Jesus and leads us in His name, is called the **visible** head of the Church or the VICAR (G) OF CHRIST. After the Pope come the bishops, who are the successors of the apostles, as the Pope is the successor of Peter.

Of course, during Jesus' public life the Church was just beginning to form. But already our Savior had begun to foretell the great growth it would have later. Once, for example, He compared it to a tiny seed which developed into such a large tree that "the birds of the air came to build their nests in its branches." When we think of the fact that today the Church is all over the world, we see that Jesus' prophecy has come true.

Peter still had much to learn before he would be ready for his special mission. He wasn't Pope yet.

Very soon after his declaration that Jesus was the Messiah, Peter found himself in trouble. This is how it happened:

Jesus began to say disturbing things: that He was going to have to suffer and be put to death. He also added that He would rise from the dead.

Peter couldn't bear to listen to this talk about suffering and dying. After all, Jesus was their leader! He was the Messiah! And—perhaps most of all—Peter couldn't stand the thought of the kind and good Jesus having to suffer.

So Peter took Him to one side and said, "May You be spared, Lord! This mustn't happen to You!"

Jesus turned and faced him squarely. "Out of my sight, you satan!" He said. "You're trying to block my path, because you think by man's standards, not God's."

Imagine how Peter must have felt! Humbly he realized that he had much to learn yet.

And imagine how Jesus felt! His chief reason for coming into the world had been to suffer and die for all mankind—yet here was Peter advising Him to take the easy, comfortable way out. Jesus was human as well as divine. The very thought of His future sufferings must have been torture to Him. So what Peter said was like a temptation, and that was why Jesus used the label "satan."

A few days after Jesus' first prediction of His passion, He took Peter, James and John up a mountain with Him. There He gave their faith a boost by letting them catch a glimpse of His divinity. His face and garments shone brightly. A cloud came down upon Him, just as a cloud had dwelt in the meeting tent of the Exodus and in the temple of Solomon. From it a voice said, "This is my beloved Son. Listen to Him."

Moses and Elijah, representing the law and prophets of the Old Testament, appeared beside Jesus and talked with Him. Surely, this scene must have encouraged the apostles—even though the conversation they overheard was about Jesus' approaching passion (G) and death.

Suggested Readings: John 6:66-71; Matthew 16:13-23; 13:31-32; Luke 9:28-36

Who is the greatest of all the saints?
The greatest of all the saints is Mary, Jesus' Mother. She used her special gifts from God in the best possible way, growing in grace and virtue throughout her life.

What did Jesus' promise to Peter mean?
Jesus' promise meant that Peter was to be the chief leader of the Church after Himself and that the Church would never be overcome.

What is infallibility?
Infallibility is a gift given by the Holy Spirit to the Pope and the bishops united with him. It means freedom from making mistakes when teaching a truth of faith or morals (right living) to the whole Church.

"Lord..., you have the words of eternal life. We have come to believe; we are convinced that you are God's holy one."
(John 6:68-69)

16 MAN FOR OTHERS

One day when Jesus was teaching, a lawyer (that is, an expert on the religious laws of the Jewish people) asked Him what we must do to gain eternal life. Jesus, in turn, asked His questioner what the law of Moses said about this. Combining a quote from Deuteronomy with another from Leviticus, the lawyer replied:

"You must love the Lord your God with all your heart, with all your soul, with all your strength, and with all your mind, and your neighbor as yourself."

(Luke 10:27)**

Jesus approved the answer.
But the lawyer pressed on. "Who **is** my neighbor?" he asked.
Jesus replied by telling what is perhaps the most famous story in the whole Bible. Its setting was a familiar one for the people to whom He was speaking: the road from Jerusalem to Jericho.
This road threads its way through barren, rocky hills, descending lower and lower from the mountains east of Jerusalem to the Jordan valley, which is below sea level. The area was uninhabited, and therefore a favorite zone for robbers, who would hide behind boulders or ridges to ambush travelers.
Said Jesus, "There was a man going down from Jerusalem to Jericho who was ambushed by robbers. They took everything he had, beat him and then went on their way, leaving him half dead. It happened that a priest came down the same road, but when he saw the man he continued on his way. The same thing took place when a Levite came along and saw him; he, too, passed by."
So far the story hadn't jarred the listeners. Maybe the priest and

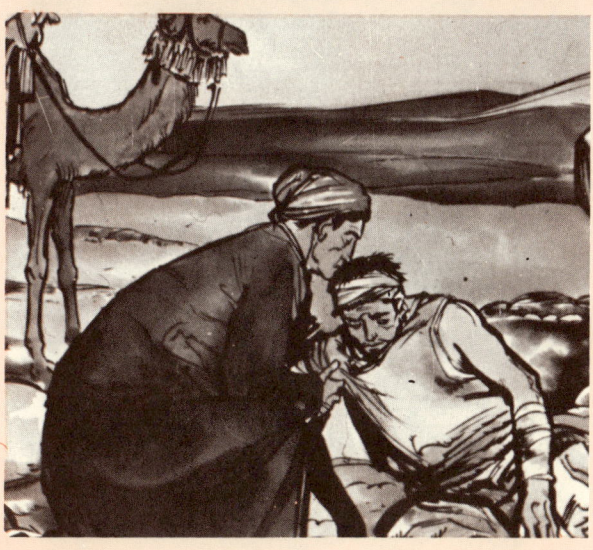

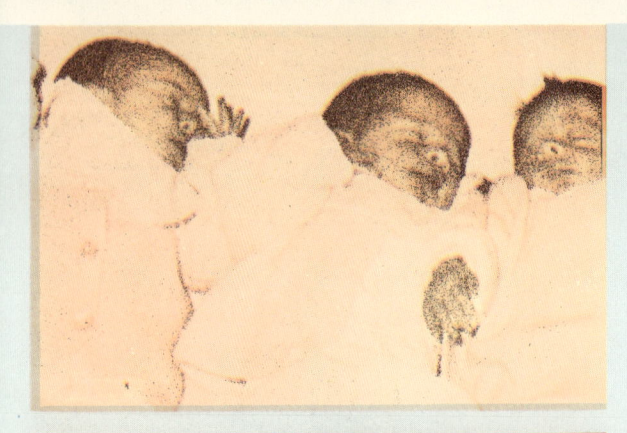

Levite were in a hurry.... Maybe they were afraid the man was a decoy for a band of robbers.... Maybe they thought he was dead anyway....

"But a Samaritan who was traveling came along and was moved with pity when he saw him...."

We can imagine the members of Jesus' audience stiffening in surprise. Jews did not like Samaritans and vice versa. This unfriendliness went back about seven hundred years—to the time when the Samaritans had first come into existence.

But Jesus calmly continued, "He went up to him and bandaged up his wounds, pouring oil and wine into them. Then, lifting him onto his own mount, he took him to an inn where he cared for him. The next day he gave the innkeeper two silver pieces, saying, 'Take care of him, and if you spend anything extra I'll repay you on my way back.'"

Jesus looked at the lawyer who had asked about his neighbor. "In your opinion," Jesus asked, "which of these three men showed himself the neighbor of the one who had been ambushed by the robbers?"

"The one who showed compassion for him." (The lawyer couldn't bring himself to say, "The Samaritan.")

"Then," concluded Jesus, "go and act the same way."

Jesus really **had** given a new meaning to the moral law as it was understood by the people of His time. For example, He taught:

"You have heard the commandment, 'You shall love your countryman but hate your enemy.' My command to you is: love your enemies, pray for your persecutors. This will prove that you are sons of your heavenly Father, for his sun rises on the bad and the good...."

(Matthew 5:43-45)*

Down through the 2,000 years of its history, the Church has tried to take to heart these teachings of Jesus—that **every** man is our neighbor, our brother.

The last great council (G) of bishops, which was called Vatican II, said this: "Everyone must consider his every neighbor without exception as another self.... In our times a special obligation binds us to make ourselves the neighbor of every person without exception, and of actively helping him when he comes across our path...."

Who are our neighbors? They include:
- the retarded
- the aged
- the unborn
- the sick
- the poor
- the suffering
- the lonely
- the sinful.

We can help these people and others by carrying out WORKS OF MERCY, such as those described by Jesus in Matthew 25:31-46. Jesus regards what we do to others as done to Him.

At the end of this textbook you will find a list of fourteen works of mercy, based on Jesus' teachings and put together by the Church.

Jesus showed His love for people by healing them in body and spirit. His followers should do the same. In the First Letter of John we read:

I ask you, how can God's love survive
  in a man
who has enough of this world's goods
yet closes his heart to his brother
when he sees him in need?
Little children,
let us love in deed and in truth
and not merely talk about it.
　　　　　　　(1 John 3:17-18)*

Each of us has something he or she can give to others, even if it's only a smile, a few words of conversation, an intention placed in our prayers.... But sometimes it can be more: working with underprivileged children, running errands for the elderly, making simple gifts for the sick, collecting canned goods and clothing for the poor, helping pro-life groups, bringing lonely boys and girls into one's own circle of friends....

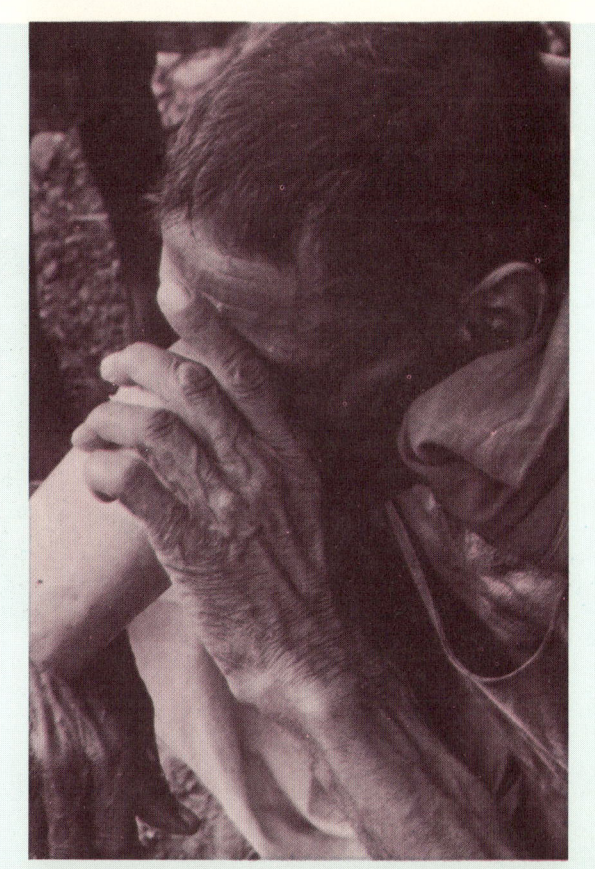

St. Luke, the only evangelist who has given us the Good Samaritan parable, follows this parable with an interesting story:

One day Jesus stopped at the home of His friends, Martha and Mary, two women who lived in Bethany, a village near Jerusalem. Probably Jesus' disciples were with Him, too, for Martha was soon very busy preparing the meal and serving it—so busy, in fact, that she complained to Jesus, "Lord, don't You care that my sister has left me all alone to do the serving? Tell her to help me."

Meanwhile, Mary was sitting at Jesus' feet, listening to Him. She didn't want to miss a word.

"Martha, Martha," said Jesus gently, "you worry and get disturbed over so many things, but really only one is necessary. Mary has chosen the better part, and it shall not be taken away from her."

Perhaps Luke placed the story of Martha and Mary right after the parable of the Good Samaritan to remind us that in doing good for others we must never forget God. After all, God is the very reason for loving others; we love others—all others—because He asks us to do so. In serving our brothers and sisters, we should do so in God's name, counting on His help.

How do we get God's help? By listening to His Word, as Mary did. By receiving Jesus in the Eucharist. By receiving the sacrament of Penance well. By PRAYING.

We pray to ask God's help for ourselves and others. Our first parents thought they didn't need God. We shouldn't make the same mistake.

We also pray for other reasons:

We pray to adore (praise) and to thank God.

We pray to ask God's forgiveness and to make up for sin.

Prayer is as important for a Christian as breathing. If we look at the life of Jesus, we'll see that. How many times in the Gospels He thanked and praised His Father! How many times His apostles found Him praying!

And Jesus urged **us** to pray, too. Here is just one example of what He said about the importance of prayer:

"I say to you, 'Ask and you shall receive; seek and you shall find; knock and it shall be opened to you.'

"For whoever asks, receives; whoever seeks, finds; whoever knocks, is admitted. What father among you will give his son a snake if he asks for a fish, or hand him a scorpion if he asks for an egg? If you, with all your sins, know how to give your children good things, how much more will the heavenly Father give the Holy Spirit to those who ask him."

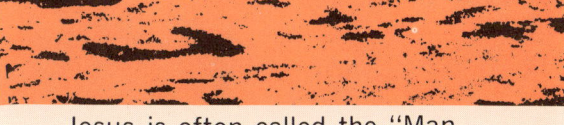

(Luke 11:9-13)*

Jesus is often called the "Man for others." Who are the "others"? First, His Father in heaven. Then, each and every one of us. As His close followers, we, too, should be "persons for others"—for God and for the whole human family. We have received many special gifts from Him, such as faith, grace, religious instruction, actual graces.... It is up to us to use them with a sense of responsibility.

Suggested Readings: Luke 10:25-37; 6:27-38; Matthew 25:31-46; Luke 10:38-42

What change did Jesus make in teachings regarding love?
Jesus taught that we are to love **everyone,** not just those who are closest to us.

What are works of mercy?
Works of mercy are good deeds done for others out of love for God and people.

What are the main reasons for praying?
The main reasons for praying are: to adore God; to thank Him; to ask His forgiveness and to make up for sin; to ask His help for ourselves and others.

Your ways, O Lord, make known to me;
 teach me your paths,
Guide me in your truth and teach me,
 for you are God my savior.

(Psalm 25:4-5)*

Unit 4 Light Battles Darkness

17
HE SPOKE UP FOR JESUS

Jerusalem was in a state of turmoil over Jesus.

Even though the first three Gospels concentrate on the Savior's mission in Galilee, we know from St. John that Jesus had been working miracles in Jerusalem, too. For this reason, a religious leader named Nicodemus came to Jesus and said:

"Rabbi, we know you are a teacher come from God, for no man can perform signs and wonders such as you perform unless God is with him."

(John 3:2)*

John tells us further that Nicodemus came to Jesus at night because he didn't want to be seen. Seen by whom? By other religious leaders. You see, they themselves were divided about Him.

To understand this strange situation, we need to realize that there were various groups in Palestine at that time, each of which had its own outlook on life and religion.

Three groups that had originated around the time of the Maccabean revolt were the Sadducees, Pharisees and Essenes.

The Sadducees were made up of most of the leading priests and wealthy laymen. They were concerned about staying on good terms with Rome, which ruled Palestine.

The Pharisees were mostly laymen. Among them were the Scribes, also called lawyers or doctors of the law. Members of this group prided themselves on obeying a great number of rules and regulations that had been developed since the time of Ezra.

The Essenes lived apart from everyone else at Qumran, near the Dead Sea, and perhaps in other isolated spots as well. They tried to prepare themselves for the coming of the Messiah (more than one Messiah, it seems) by leading good lives and repenting of their sins.

The Zealots were a political group, chiefly composed of Galileans, who wanted to revolt against Rome.

And then there were the common people.

How did all these people feel about the Messiah? In different ways. And this was why some people accepted Jesus while others did not. Those who were looking for an earthly king or the leader of a revolt against Rome didn't find their Messiah. But those who wanted someone to bring them closer to God **did** find their Messiah. They recognized Jesus as the One sent by God.

A common complaint against Jesus was that He healed sick people on the Sabbath (G). This was against the regulations laid down by the Pharisees, and, of course, the Pharisees were the ones who made this complaint. The Pharisees were also alarmed because of Jesus' popularity with the common people.

And they were especially disturbed by this: Jesus forgave sins in His own name, which only God can do. And He called God His own Father! He even had the courage to say:

"I solemnly declare it:
before Abraham came to be, I AM."
(John 8:58)*

"I am," of course, was the name of Yahweh.

It may have been an autumn day in the year 29 A.D. when Jesus and His disciples passed by a young beggar who had been blind from birth.

"Rabbi," the disciples asked, "was this man born blind because he sinned or because his parents sinned?" (In those times, it was a common belief that every handicap was a punishment for sin.)

"Neither," replied Jesus. "He was born blind so God's works could be shown in him. While the day lasts we must do the work of the One who sent me. The night is coming, and then no one can work. As long as I am in the world I am the light of the world."

Then Jesus spat on the ground, made mud with the saliva, and spread the mud on the blind man's eyes. He had worked other miracles in this way before. (It was not an unusual method, for saliva was believed to have healing qualities.)

"Go and wash in the pool of Siloam," Jesus told the blind man.

The beggar went down to the pool, located in the southeastern section of Jerusalem. He washed and came away seeing.

People noticed this right away, and once they were sure that he was the same man who used to sit and beg they took him to the Pharisees.

It was the Sabbath day.

"This man can't be from God!" exclaimed some of the Pharisees, speaking of Jesus. "He doesn't keep the Sabbath."

But others said, "How could a sinner work such wonders?"

So they turned to the beggar and asked **his** opinion.

"He's a prophet," said the man born blind.

The situation was embarrassing for the Pharisees. "Perhaps this man wasn't really born blind," said one of them. "Let's send for his parents and ask them."

So they did.

"Is this man your son?" they asked. "Was he really born blind? If so, why is he able to see now?"

"We know that he's our own son," replied the parents. "And we know that he was born blind. Yet we don't know why he's able to see now, or who opened his eyes. But he is of age; ask him."

So the Pharisees tried again. "Give glory to God," they said to the beggar This meant, "Take an oath to tell only the truth."

"For ourselves," they continued, "we know that this man is a sinner." (They meant that Jesus had broken their Sabbath regulations. This they considered sinful.)

"I don't know whether or not he's a sinner," replied the man born blind. He knew better than to get into a legal discussion with these people! "All I know is this: I was blind and now I can see."

"What did he do to you?"

"How did he open your eyes?"

"I've told you once already, but you wouldn't listen to me. Why do you want to hear it all over again?"

The beggar wasn't going to give any evidence that they could use against Jesus. Rather, he turned the tables on his questioners by asking, "Do you want to become his disciples, too?"

That did it. "Maybe **you're** his disciple," they retorted, "but **we're** disciples of Moses. We know that

God spoke to Moses, but we don't even know where this man came from."

"That's really amazing," said the beggar. "You don't know where he's from, and yet he opened my eyes." And as if he were seeing more and more clearly into the truth, he continued, "We know that God doesn't listen to sinners but that He listens to those who worship and obey Him. Now, for someone to give sight to a person blind from birth is unheard of. Unless he were from God, this man couldn't have done such a thing."

The Pharisees were furious. "Here you are, a sinner from your birth, and are you trying to teach us? Out!"

Word of what had happened reached Jesus, who went to look for the courageous beggar. When He found him, He asked, "Do you believe in the Son of Man?" (Jesus liked to use this name for Himself, because it hid His identity quite a bit. It could be taken to mean simply "man." Yet in the Book of Daniel it had been used to describe Someone who came on the clouds of heaven and received kingship over the whole world.)

"Who is He, sir, so that I may believe in Him?"

"You have seen Him. He is speaking to you now."

"I believe, Lord," the beggar replied. His faith had grown from the moment his eyes had been opened.

And with the Pharisees it was just the opposite. As Jesus tried to tell them, they **thought** they knew the truth, so they would not accept the **real** truth. If only they had recognized their spiritual blindness, they could have asked for light and help.

In all the Gospels, but especially in that of St. John, we find deep, rich meanings that are connected with the life of the early Christian community as it developed under the Holy Spirit's guidance. In John's Gospel, we see a close relationship between the seven "signs" (miracles) that are described and the seven "signs" that are our Christian SACRAMENTS.

What is a sacrament? It is an action of Jesus, a visible sign of His invisible grace. The sacraments are the chief ways in which our Savior gives us His Spirit to make us holy.

The Holy Spirit gives us GRACE; this is what makes us HOLY (close to God). Grace is a sharing in God's own life. When describing Himself as the Good Shepherd shortly after His cure of the blind beggar, Jesus said:

"I have come
so that they (the sheep) may have life
and have it to the full."
(John 10:10)**

The life He was speaking about is grace.

Are **all** the sacraments suggested in St. John's Gospel? No, chiefly two. These are BAPTISM, the most necessary sacrament, and the EUCHARIST, which is the greatest sacrament in itself because it **is** Jesus.

The changing of the water into wine and the multiplication of the loaves both remind us of the Eucharist. The story of the man born blind may remind us of Baptism. The blind man had never **seen** before in all his life. He washed and he saw. A new life began for him. He could do things he had never done before.

In Baptism, besides grace, we receive faith, which helps us begin to "see" the things of God. At Baptism a new life began for **us,** too.

A baptized Christian should have the courage to stand up for his or her faith, just as that grateful beggar stood up for his belief in the goodness of Jesus.

Suggested Readings: John 9:1 — 10:21

Did everyone at Jesus' time agree as to what the Messiah would be like?
No. In fact, many thought that the Messiah would be a political leader.

What are the sacraments?
The sacraments are actions of Jesus—the chief ways in which He gives us His Spirit to make us holy. They are visible signs of His invisible grace.

> In the beginning was the Word;
> the Word was in God's presence,
> and the Word was God.
> He was present to God in the beginning.
> Through him all things came into being,
> and apart from him nothing came to be.
> Whatever came to be in him, found life,
> life for the light of men.
> The light shines on in darkness,
> a darkness that did not overcome it.
> He was in the world,
> and through him the world was made,
> yet the world did not know who he was.
> To his own he came,
> yet his own did not accept him.
> Any who did accept him
> he empowered to become children of God.
>
> (John 1:1-5, 10-12)*

18 LIFE RESTORED —DEATH DECREED

It was winter, probably in the year 30 A.D.

Jesus and His disciples had gone into Perea, the district of Palestine east of the Jordan, where they could feel more secure. As Jesus healed and preached, crowds again began to flock to Him. Not long before, John the Baptizer had preached in this region. John was dead now, because of the scheming of King Herod's wife. But the people remembered him well and declared, "John never worked any miracles, but everything he said about **this** man was true."

One day someone brought Jesus word from Martha and Mary, His good friends in Bethany. The message was brief and simple: "Lord, the one that You love is sick."

They meant their brother Lazarus.

"This sickness is not to end in death," said Jesus, "but rather in the glory of God. Through it the Son of God will be glorified."

The disciples may have been surprised that Jesus stayed two more days in Perea instead of hurrying back into Judea to see His sick friend. But when Jesus **did** say, "Let's go back into Judea," the concern of His followers had lessened so much that they protested, "Rabbi, not long ago they wanted to stone You, and You're going back there again?" To the disciples' way of thinking, Bethany was far too close to Jerusalem. In December, during the feast of the Dedication, some men had been ready to stone Jesus to death right there in the temple area for declaring that He and the Father were one.

But Jesus answered His disciples' objections by saying that it wasn't yet time for Him to die.

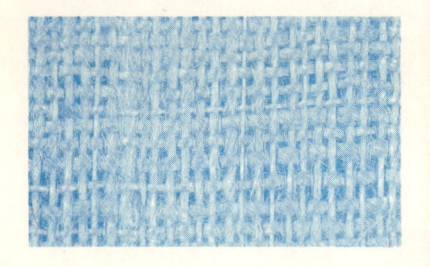

"Lazarus is dead," Jesus continued, "and for your sakes I am happy that I wasn't there, so that you may believe."

Believe? Believe what?

"At any rate," continued Jesus, "let us go to him."

"Let's go," Thomas said to the others, "and die with Him." The apostles had their brave moments, even though these didn't last long.

Soon Jesus and His disciples were trudging up the familiar, desolate road from Jericho to Jerusalem. That road eventually brought them close to Bethany, located on the eastern slope of the Mount of Olives two miles east of the Holy City.

Before they even reached the village, Martha came hurrying down the road toward them.

"Lord," she exclaimed, "if You had been here, my brother wouldn't have died." This was not a complaint, for even if Jesus had come at once it still would have been too late. Probably Martha was repeating a reflection that she and her sister had shared.

"Your brother will rise," Jesus replied gently.

"Yes, I know," said Martha, "on the last day, at the resurrection." She knew the teaching of the Pharisees that the dead would one day rise.

But Jesus indicated that He meant something else. He said:

"I am the resurrection.
If anyone believes in me, even
    though he dies he will live,
and whoever lives and believes in me
will never die."

(John 11:25-26)**

Martha drank in the words, and when Jesus asked, "Do you believe this?" she made an act of faith:

"Yes, Lord," she said. "I believe that you are the Christ, the Son of God, the one who was to come into this world."

(John 11:27)**

How pleased Jesus must have been!

Knowing that her sister would want to see Jesus, Martha hurried up the hill to call her.

When Mary came, followed by a crowd of mourners, she dropped to the ground at Jesus' feet. "Lord," she said, repeating her sister's words, "if You had been here, my brother wouldn't have died." Tears glistened in her eyes.

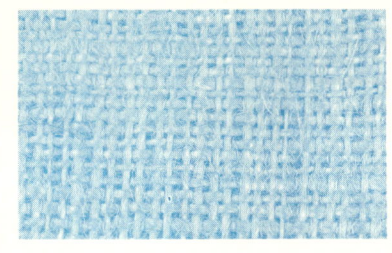

Seeing Mary and the other mourners, Jesus trembled with emotion. "Where have you placed him?" He asked. As the sisters began to lead Him toward the tomb, He, too, started to weep.

"How much he loved him!" someone exclaimed.

And someone else murmured, "Couldn't he have prevented this man from dying? After all, he opened the eyes of that blind man."

Still trembling with emotion, Jesus approached the tomb. He knew well that what He was about to do would lead to His own death.

The tomb was a cave hollowed out of the rock, with a large stone laid across the opening.

"Take the stone away," Jesus directed.

Martha—who was always practical —objected. Thinking that Jesus simply wanted to take a last look at His departed friend, she pointed out, "Lord, it has been four days already. By now there will be a smell."

"But didn't I tell you," replied Jesus, "that if you believe you will see God's glory?"

Some men moved the stone aside, revealing a dark hole with steps going downward into the blackness.

Jesus raised His eyes and prayed:

"Father, I thank you for having
 heard me.
I know that you always hear me
but I have said this for the sake
 of the crowd,
that they may believe that you
 sent me."

(John 11:41-42)*

And then, standing at the entrance of the cave, He called in a loud voice, "Come out, Lazarus!"

There was a rustling and bumping inside the cave. The crowd gasped. All wrapped in bandages, a human figure came struggling up the steps into the light of day. At the cave's entrance it stopped and stood still, unable to free itself from its wrappings.

Everyone was too stunned to move. Jesus Himself had to remind them about what to do.

"Untie him," He said. "Set him free."

Lazarus had a second chance at life. And that makes us reflect about DEATH and what follows it.

Until Jesus' time, people weren't sure about death. Throughout the Old Testament, God had revealed the fact of a next life only gradually. People who were familiar with the books of Daniel, 2 Maccabees and Wisdom understood that there would be a RESURRECTION of the dead and that those who had lived well would be in peace.

Jesus taught more about these matters. He taught of a place of eternal punishment for those who knowingly and deliberately turn away from God and never come back to Him, and of a place of everlasting life and happiness for those who live as He asks us to live. (See, for example, Matthew 25:34, 41, 46.)

Under the guidance of the Holy Spirit, the Church has come to understand (from Scripture and Tradition) that beyond the grave there is also a place of purification in which souls become more worthy to see God and live with Him.

So there are three possibilities for us after death and judgment: HEAVEN, PURGATORY or HELL.

The one we should be most interested in is heaven. It is so far beyond our wildest imaginings that we could never have done anything to deserve it. But God will give it to us if we die with His grace, which makes us His children and friends. Grace is His gift. It was won for us by Jesus at the cost of the greatest sufferings anyone on earth has ever endured.

The raising of Lazarus was at least Jesus' third miracle of bringing someone back from the dead. But this was the first time that the Savior had raised anyone to life in Judea, the center of His opposition.

Some of those who had seen the miracle were so excited that they couldn't help letting word get out to the Pharisees. And the Pharisees told the chief priests, so they could gather to discuss the matter. Why such alarm? Their line of reasoning was this: "If we leave this man alone and let him go on doing these things, the whole world will believe in him. Then the Romans will come and destroy our holy place and our people." One of them had the solution. "Can't you see," he asked, "that it's better for one man to die than for the whole nation to be destroyed?" So they began to make their plans.

Of course, Jesus knew what was going to take place. In fact, this was why He had come into the world—to give His life for us. Not because He **had** to, for He didn't **have** to save us by dying. In fact, He didn't **have** to save us at all. But out of love for us and hatred for sin, He chose to give His life.

Jesus had even selected the time that He would let Himself be taken—Passover time, for He is the **true** paschal lamb. So after the raising of Lazarus He and His disciples left the neighborhood of Jerusalem. They returned just before the feast.

What a great day **that** was! Jesus and His disciples came over the Mount of Olives accompanied by a crowd, many of whom had seen Him raise Lazarus from the dead. Jesus was riding...a war horse? No, a donkey, as the prophet Zechariah had foretold of the Messiah. He was not coming as a political ruler or military leader, but as the meek, humble Lord of a spiritual kingdom.

A second enthusiastic crowd greeted Him as He proceeded down into the Kidron valley and then up the slope leading to the city. Many pilgrims had already arrived for the feast. Joyful over the raising of Lazarus, they came out from the city, waving branches and shouting, "Hosanna!" (which means: Save us, O Lord!) "Blessed is the King of Israel, who comes in the name of the Lord!"

"Look!" the Pharisees said to one another, "the whole world has gone running after him!"

Suggested Readings: John 11:1—12:19

What awaits a person after death and judgment?
　　After death and judgment, a person may go to heaven for all eternity; he may go to purgatory temporarily and then to heaven; or he may go to hell for all eternity.

"Yes, God loved the world so much
that he gave his only Son,
so that everyone who believes in him may not be lost
but may have eternal life.
For God sent his Son into the world
not to condemn the world,
but so that through him the world might be saved."

(John 3:16-17)**

19
NO LIMITS TO LOVE

We cannot be absolutely sure about this, but probably it was a Thursday at Passover time in the year 30 A.D. If this is true, the date was April 6.

That particular morning Jesus was not in the city. Perhaps He and His disciples had spent the night on the slopes of the Mount of Olives. There was a garden there where He often liked to pray. Or perhaps they had gone over the mount to Bethany, where, as we know, Jesus had friends.

In any event, they would go to Jerusalem that evening to celebrate the Passover.

"Where shall we prepare the Passover supper for You?" the disciples asked. Jesus fixed His gaze on Peter and John. "When you enter the city," He said, "you will see a man carrying a jar of water. Follow him home and say to the house's owner, 'The Teacher asks: Do you have a guest room in which I may eat the Passover with my disciples?' He will show you an upstairs room, large and furnished. Prepare it there."

A man (rather than a woman) carrying a water jar was quite an unusual sight in Palestine. So the man Jesus had mentioned was easy for Peter and John to find and follow. (The owner of the house was not at all surprised by the disciples' request, since residents of Jerusalem normally offered a banquet room to pilgrims who had come to celebrate the Passover.)

Peter and John saw to the arrangement of the furniture—couches placed next to the table at an angle. It was customary to eat while lying on one's side, propped up on one elbow.

The two apostles also obtained or prepared the needed provisions: a salad of bitter herbs; unleavened bread (G); wine; and a sauce made of wine, fruits and nuts. A lamb was purchased and taken to the temple to be slaughtered. Then the apostles roasted it outdoors on a spit and brought it to the supper room.

As usual, John tells us different facts about the Last Supper than the other three evangelists do. For this reason, and also because the Gospels say very little about this Passover meal itself, we really can't be sure of the order in which the events took place. But since the structure of the Passover meal is known, what happened may have been something like this:

First Jesus, as leader of the group, blessed a cup of wine and passed it around for all to drink from. At the same time, He told them:

"I have greatly desired to eat this Passover with you before I suffer."

(Luke 22:15)*

Yet somehow the apostles soon forgot that this was a special moment. It wasn't long before they were arguing among themselves as to which of them was the most important.

THE CITY OF JERUSALEM

Here St. Stephen was martyred

Pool of Bethesda
where Jesus cured a paralytic

Sheep Gate

Roman Fortress of Antonia

Gethsemane

Holy Sepulchre
Calvary

THE TEMPLE

Mt. Moria

Sanhedrin

Palace of Maccabean Dynasty (Hasmoneans)

Praetorium of Pilate?

Kidron Valley
which Jesus and His disciples often crossed on the way to Bethany or Gethsemane

Gardens

UPPER CITY

Home of Caiphas

LOWER CITY

Mt. Zion

Cenacle, the traditional site of the Last Supper and Pentecost

Pool of Siloam to which Jesus sent a blind man to be cured

north / west / east / south

Ge-hinnom
where the bodies of criminals were burned

Akeldama

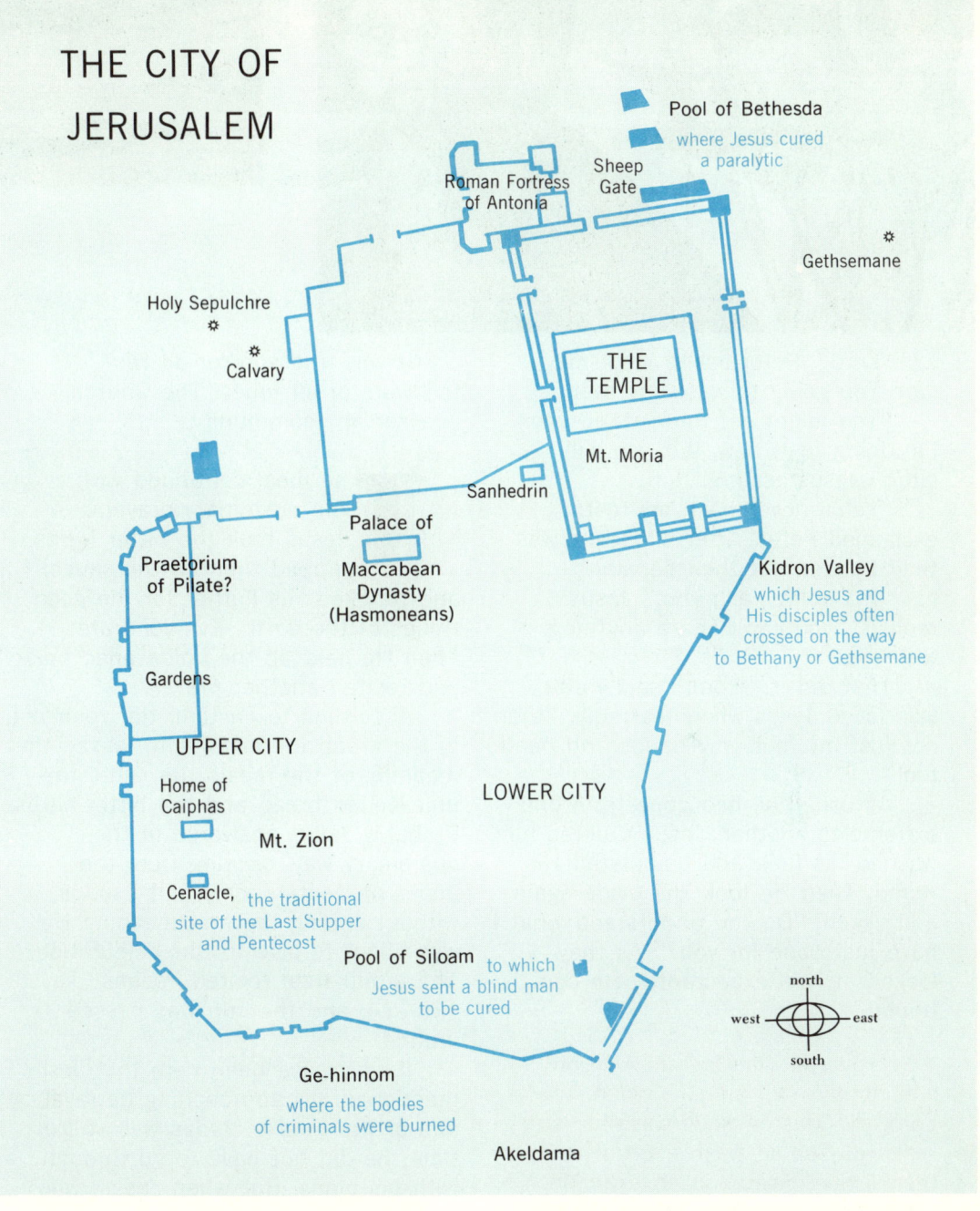

Jesus had caught them doing this before. Now He taught them a lesson with His own example.

Everyone had just washed his hands, a normal part of the ceremony. Jesus stood up, tied a towel around His waist with the ends hanging free, and began to go from one to another of His apostles as they reclined on their couches. He washed their feet, as a slave would have done, drying them with the free ends of the towel that was wrapped around Him. In due course He came to Peter.

91

"Lord," Peter asked in dismay, "are You going to wash my feet?"

"You might not understand what I'm doing right now, but you will later," Jesus assured him.

"You'll never wash **my** feet!" exclaimed Peter. After all, Jesus was their Leader, not their servant.

"If I don't wash you," Jesus replied, "you can't share anything with me."

That did it. "Lord," said Peter, who loved Jesus wholeheartedly, "then not just my feet—my hands and head too!"

As usual, he had gone from one extreme to another. Jesus quieted him, washed his feet, and completed His round. Then He took His place again and asked, "Do you understand what I have just done for you?" As they looked at Him expectantly, He continued:

"You call me Master and Lord, and rightly; so I am. If I, then, the Lord and Master, have washed your feet, you should wash each other's feet. I have given you an example so that you may copy what I have done to you.

"I tell you most solemnly,
no servant is greater than his master,
no messenger is greater than the man who sent him."

It was a lesson for all His followers of all times. The Church is a servant community.

The meal continued with the customary prayers. Jesus took the bitter herbs, dipped them in the sauce, and thanked His Father for the good things of the earth. Everyone ate. Then He held up the unleavened bread and recited another prayer.

According to custom, the youngest in the group (perhaps John) asked the meaning of the meal—the lamb, the unleavened bread and the bitter herbs. Probably Jesus answered in the customary way, quoting from the books of Deuteronomy and Exodus, without adding the new meaning He was about to give to this celebration. The group then recited Psalms 113-114, and the cup was passed around.

It may have been here that Jesus mentioned His approaching betrayal by one of the Twelve. Judas was still in time; he did not have to go through with his plans. But when Jesus, who knew Judas' heart, saw that the man was determined to hand Him over to the Pharisees and Sadducees, He told him, "Be quick about what you're going to do."

(John 13:13-16)**

The other apostles did not understand. As Judas left the table and hurried out into the night, some thought he had been sent on an errand.

Perhaps it was now that Jesus took the unleavened bread, which He had not yet distributed, and fulfilled that momentous promise He had made during another Passover season:

Then, taking bread and giving thanks, he broke it and gave it to them, saying: "This is my body to be given for you. Do this as a remembrance of me."

(Luke 22:19)*

Do the same in His memory! Although they might not have realized it, the apostles had become priests! The greatest power of the priest is that of changing bread and wine into the Body and Blood of Christ in His name.

After the group had eaten the paschal lamb, Jesus prepared a cup of wine, called the "cup of blessing." Again, He transformed it:

He did the same with the cup after eating, saying as he did so: "This cup is the new covenant in my blood, which will be shed for you...."

(Luke 22:20)*

Did the apostles realize what was taking place? Jesus was giving them His **all**. And a new covenant between God and man was coming into being. As the blood sprinkled at Sinai had represented the people's closeness to God and one another, far more so the cup shared at the Last Supper showed the oneness of the apostles with God, for God came within them.

At the end of the Passover meal, the rest of the customary psalms (115-118) were recited. The last of them has become a favorite Easter psalm of the Church.

The Last Supper looked back over the centuries to God's great saving action in the EXODUS. It looked forward to the **greatest** of all God's saving actions —Jesus' DEATH and RESURRECTION.

Jesus was about to lay down His life for each and every one of us. And He had now given His apostles the way to bring His sacrifice into the lives of people of every time and place, so that all of us could be present at it and join Him in His offering. In the MASS the priest speaks for Jesus, who offers His sacrifice again.

Besides being a renewal of the sacrifice of the cross, the Mass is also a memorial (remembering) of Jesus' death, resurrection and ascension. It is a holy covenant meal in which we receive our Savior Himself, thus growing closer to Him and His people.

The wonderful gift of the Eucharist is only for **believers,** and this is probably why the first part of the Mass is about our belief. In the LITURGY OF THE WORD, God speaks to us through the Scriptures. We reply to Him by saying that wonderful prayer, the Profession of Faith (or Creed).

Then the LITURGY OF THE EUCHARIST begins. We offer ourselves to the Father, and when Jesus becomes present on the altar at the Consecration, we offer Him and ourselves with Him. We do this for four purposes: to adore (praise) God, to thank Him, to ask His forgiveness and atone (make up) for sin, and to ask His help for ourselves and others.

The Communion part of the Mass is a celebration of love. Jesus comes to us to make us more like Himself. We should plan to go out from Mass eager to bring His love to others, especially to those in greatest need.

Suggested Readings: John 13:1-31; Luke 22:7-20

What was the Last Supper?
   The Last Supper was the meal at which Jesus gave us the greatest gift possible —His very self.

What is the Mass?
   The Mass is:
   —The sacrifice of the cross taking place on our altars
   —A memorial of Jesus' death, resurrection and ascension
   —A holy covenant meal in which we receive Jesus Himself.

What are the main purposes of the Mass?
   The main purposes of the Mass are:
   —To adore (praise) God
   —To thank Him
   —To ask His forgiveness and atone (make up) for sin
   —To ask His help for ourselves and others.

> His state was divine,
> yet he did not cling
> to his equality with God
> but emptied himself
> to assume the condition of a slave,
> and became as men are;
> and being as all men are,
> he was humbler yet,
> even to accepting death,
> death on a cross.
>
> (Philippians 2:6-8)**

20 A GLIMPSE OF WORLDS BEYOND

St. John's Gospel gives us a glimpse into the heart of our Savior that could only have been written by someone who loved Jesus deeply. To this Gospel we owe most of our knowledge of Jesus' last words to His chosen ones before His passion (G) and death.

Some of these words were spoken at the Last Supper. Others may have been uttered on the way to the Garden of Gethsemani, and perhaps a few were said at other times and in other places.

Several themes keep repeating themselves throughout chapters 13 to 17 of John, but one fact especially stands out—love, the overwhelming love of Jesus for His chosen ones, the overwhelming love of Jesus for us.

Jesus had first washed the feet of His disciples, even though, as Peter himself protested, the apostles were unworthy of this. Then Jesus had made them priests and had given Himself to them in holy Communion, even though—again—no human being is worthy of such honors.

Now, on that chill spring evening, by the light of flickering torches in the upper room, He continued to give them everything He could.

What they needed most was encouragement, for He knew how the events of His passion and death would shake their faith, shatter their hopes and all but break their hearts. So He began to encourage them, and from the way He spoke we can see how tender was the relationship between Him and them:

"My children, I am not to be with
   you much longer.
You will look for me,
but I say to you now...
'Where I am going, you cannot come.'"
                            (John 13:33)*

At once Peter wanted to know where Jesus intended to go, and Jesus told him, "For now, I'm going where you cannot follow me, but later on you shall."

"Lord," Peter protested, "why can't I follow You now? Why, I would lay down my life for You!"

"Oh, would you?" replied Jesus. "Simon, Simon, you must know that Satan has asked for you. He wants to sift all of you like wheat. But I have prayed for you, Simon, so that your faith may never fail. When you have recovered you must strengthen your brothers.... Before the cock crows today, you will have three times denied that you know me."

Jesus knew everything—knew that the apostles would scatter as He was being led away from Gethsemani, knew that Peter would disown Him three times, knew that Judas had already begun to gather men to take Him prisoner.

Yet He was not bitter. Rather, He was worried about His Eleven. How sad and frightened they were going to be! Again, He tried to encourage them:

"Do not let your hearts be troubled.
Have faith in God
and faith in me.
In my Father's house there are many
    dwelling places;
otherwise, how could I have told you
that I am going to prepare a place
    for you?
I am indeed going to prepare a place
    for you,
and then I shall come back to take
    you with me,
that where I am you also may be."
(John 14:1-3)*

Later the apostles would treasure these words, knowing that there truly was a place waiting for them in the kingdom of the Father. Jesus added:

"You know the way that leads
    where I go."
(John 14:4)*

At this Thomas asked, "Lord, we don't know where You are going, so how can we know the way?"
Jesus replied:

"I am the way, and the truth,
    and the life."
(John 14:6)*

It was a beautiful definition. As God, Jesus is absolute TRUTH. As God He is also LIFE itself— "He Who Is"—Yahweh. And as the God-man, He is our WAY, or path, to the Father. To live as Jesus lived is to become perfect and "earn" a place in the Father's house.

Jesus loved to speak about His Father. As He began to do so now, Philip exclaimed, "Lord, if You show us the Father, we'll be satisfied."

We can imagine that Jesus sighed. After everything He had said and done to reveal His identity, these chosen men of His still didn't understand that He and the Father were one. But patiently He told them so again:

"To have seen me is to have seen the
    Father,
so how can you say, 'Let us see the
    Father'?
Do you not believe
that I am in the Father and the
    Father is in me?"
(John 14:9-10)**

Unless they remembered this, the events of the next few hours would be shattering for them indeed.

Jesus continued with His words of encouragement, asking them to believe in Him, promising them that if they asked for anything in His name He would do it.

And then He spoke of Someone else:

"I shall ask the Father,
and he will give you another
    Advocate
to be with you for ever,
that Spirit of truth
whom the world can never receive
since it neither sees nor knows him;
but you know him,
because he is with you, he is in you."
(John 14:16-17)**

"Advocate" (or "Paraclete") has many possible meanings, such as mediator (G) or support. Who was this Person, the Spirit of truth, whom Jesus described as being with and in the apostles? The early Church called Him the Holy Spirit, or simply the Spirit, and these are the names by which we know Him best today.

THE TEMPLE OF JERUSALEM

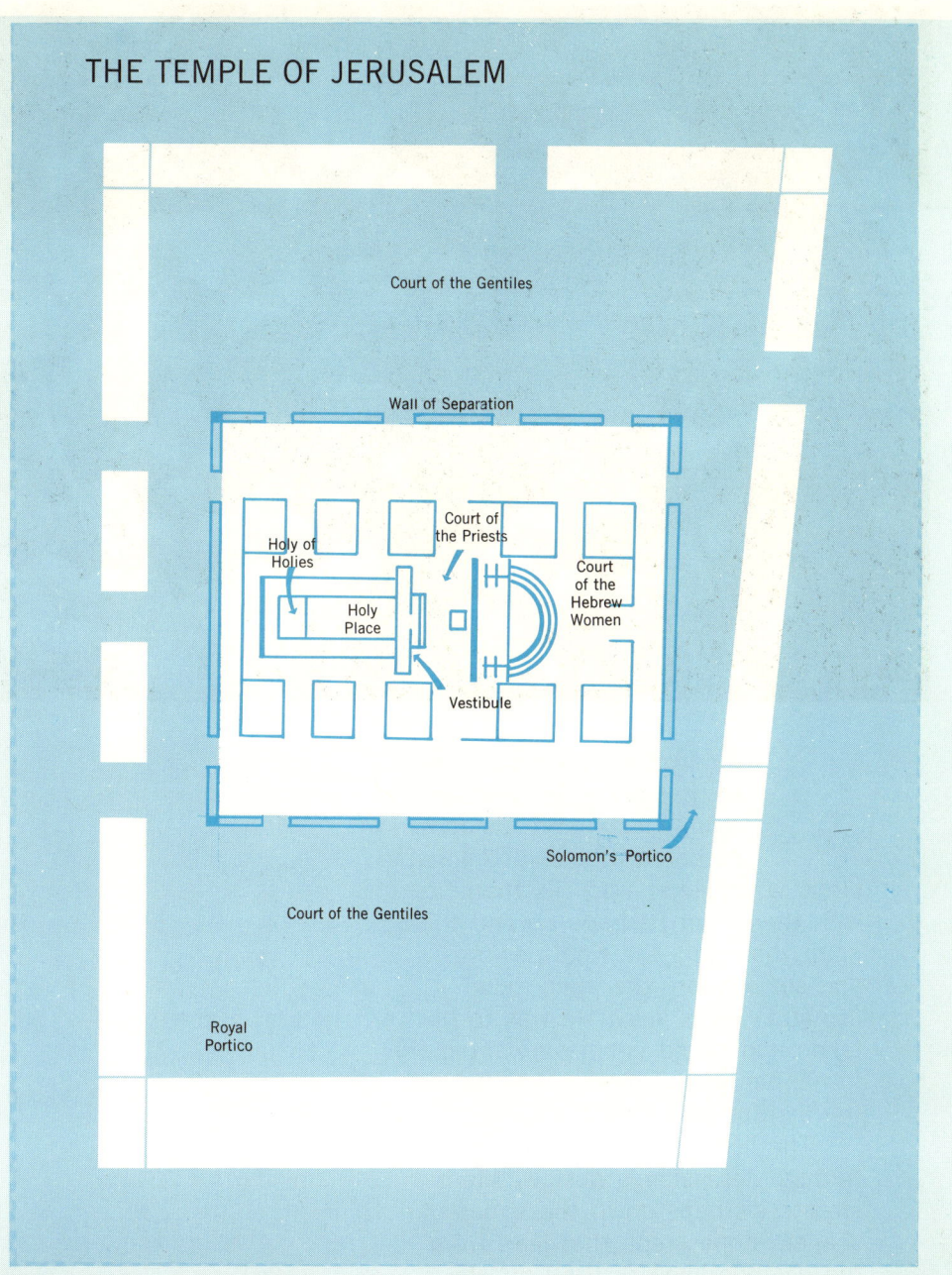

- Court of the Gentiles
- Wall of Separation
- Holy of Holies
- Court of the Priests
- Holy Place
- Court of the Hebrew Women
- Vestibule
- Solomon's Portico
- Court of the Gentiles
- Royal Portico

Jesus had gradually revealed the great and amazing mystery that while there is only ONE GOD (one divine nature) there are THREE DIVINE PERSONS. Each of these Persons is God. Each possesses the whole divine nature. Together, the Father, Son and Holy Spirit form a wonderful community of love—a community that wants to share its love and truth with us:

"Anybody who receives my commandments and keeps them
will be one who loves me;
and anybody who loves me will be loved by my Father....
and we shall come to him
and make our home with him....
I have said these things to you
while still with you;
but the Advocate, the Holy Spirit,
whom the Father will send in my name,
will teach you everything
and remind you of all I have said to you."

(John 14:21, 23, 25-26)**

We might picture the warmth of that scene in the upper room—Jesus and His apostles gathered in a companionable circle while He shared His thoughts with them. But perhaps around this point they sang the final psalms and set out into the chill, moonlit night. Jesus knew He was to be taken and would not have wanted this to happen in the room made holy by the institution of the Eucharist.

The little group made its way through Jerusalem's narrow, silent streets, perhaps down the series of shallow stone steps that lead from the neighborhood of the Cenacle (the upper room) to the Pool of Siloam, and then on down through the Kidron valley.

Perhaps they passed by a vineyard, whose vine stocks and young shoots could be seen clearly in the light of the paschal (G) moon.

Israel itself had been compared to a vine in Psalm 80 and in the prophecies of Ezekiel and Jeremiah. Now Jesus took this comparison and gave it a new and very beautiful meaning:

"I am the true vine,
and my Father is the vinedresser....
Make your home in me, as I make mine in you.
As a branch cannot bear fruit all by itself,
but must remain part of the vine,
neither can you unless you remain in me.
I am the vine,
you are the branches.
Whoever remains in me, with me in him,
bears fruit in plenty;
for cut off from me you can do nothing...."

(John 15:1, 4-5)**

With these words He clearly showed that wonderful relationship with Him that we have by the grace He was about to win for us—a relationship which will last, if we live as He wishes us to live. By grace (and, of course, through the Eucharist, which **is** Jesus, the Cause of grace) we are one with Him. And, being one with Him, we are one with each other—with all God's people on earth, in heaven and in purgatory. This great reality of oneness is sometimes called the MYSTICAL BODY of Christ, an expression used by St. Paul. The members of the mystical body are able to help one another by prayer. This giving of help is sometimes called the communion of saints.

If we read the **whole** passage on the vine and branches (John 15:1-17), we see clearly what a great love Jesus had for His apostles. And in the passages that follow this our Savior continues to encourage His chosen ones. Jesus' prayer for unity (oneness) in chapter 17 is especially beautiful. In it He asks His Father to protect His chosen ones from evil and to keep them united to Himself and one another.

This was to be the very purpose of His approaching passion and death—to make peace between His Father and mankind, and to make peace among men themselves, so that all of us might share true life and everlasting joy.

Suggested Readings: Luke 22:31-34; John 13:33—15:17

What is the mystery of the blessed Trinity?
The mystery of the blessed Trinity means that there is only one God, and in God there are three divine Persons—the Father, the Son and the Holy Spirit.

How are we united to Jesus?
We are united to Jesus like branches to the vine by the divine life of grace.

What is the communion of saints?
The communion of saints is the communication of spiritual help among the members of Christ's body (the Church) in heaven, on earth and in purgatory.

"Father, the hour has come:
glorify your Son
so that your Son may glorify you;
and, through the power over all mankind that you have given him,
let him give eternal life to all those you have entrusted to him...."

(John 17:1-2)**

21 THE MYSTERIOUS VICTORY

Only the occasional shriek of a jackal and the harsh laugh of a hyena broke the stillness. The olive groves appeared as dark patches on the moonlit hills, while here and there in more open spaces a pilgrim's campfire gleamed, as men sat before their tents and talked far into the night.

Jesus and His disciples were walking along the road ascending the Mount of Olives. Beyond a low, stone wall lay an olive grove—the Garden of Gethsemani—which doubtless belonged to one of Jesus' friends. They stopped at the gate.

"Stay here," He told the group, "while I go in and pray." But He beckoned Peter, James and John to accompany Him. These three had been strengthened by the vision of His glory on the mountaintop. Thus, they should have been better able to bear up under what was about to take place.

Peter was startled by the change that had come over Jesus. By the light of an occasional moonbeam sifting down through the trees, he could see hesitancy in His walk, furrows in His brow, utter dread in His eyes. Peter had never seen the Master like this!

After leading the three a short distance into the garden, Jesus stopped. As if in a daze, He murmured, "My heart is sorrowful to the breaking point. Wait here and stay awake with me."

The three disciples watched their leader walk—almost stagger—a few feet farther on and throw Himself to the ground in prayer. They could hear His words as He choked them out one by one: "Father, you can do all things. If it is your will, remove this cup from me. Yet your will, not mine be done."

The disciples tried to pray, too. They had never seen anyone shaken by such sorrow. But their own sadness seemed to numb them, and then sleep provided an escape....

"Simon!" It was Jesus' voice, calling Peter by his old name. "Simon, are you sleeping? Couldn't you stay awake for even an hour? Wake up and pray not to give in to temptation."

But even in His own sorrow—far greater than any other sorrow in the world, because He could see before Him all the sins of all time—Jesus found an excuse for His followers. "The spirit is willing," He added. "It's nature that is weak."

Jesus returned to His place of prayer and again begged the Father to remove the suffering from Him if He willed to do so.

The disciples again tried to pray, and again dozed off....

A second time Jesus roused them, and then a third. But the third time was the last, for the Master declared that now they should be on their way. "See," He said, "my betrayer is close by."

The disciples struggled to their feet and peered toward the road. Lanterns and torches flickering between the trees showed that a good-sized crowd was approaching the gate.

Bewildered, Peter looked at the Master and suddenly realized that Jesus' face, hands and garments were drenched with perspiration and blood. What had He been through tonight? Yet Jesus' old, calm manner had returned. The dread had vanished from His eyes, and as He led them out to the gate His step was sure.

Peter couldn't believe it; everything had happened so suddenly. Jesus—the good and gentle Jesus—had been taken prisoner and led off bound to the home of Annas, father-in-law of the high priest. And Peter himself? First, he had made an attempt to save his Master. Pulling out a sword that he wore concealed beneath his cloak, he had lunged at one of the high priest's servants and slashed off his ear. Yet Jesus had picked up the ear, restored it to its place, and healed the man!

Now, having fled into the darkness, Peter was following cautiously from a distance. From the house of Annas, Jesus was taken to that of Caiaphas, the official high priest. Peter hung along behind, looking for an opportunity to draw closer. At last the chance came. As Jesus entered the high priest's courtyard, one of His disciples, who knew some of the servants, also entered. After a few minutes this disciple spoke to the maidservant at the gate and motioned Peter in.

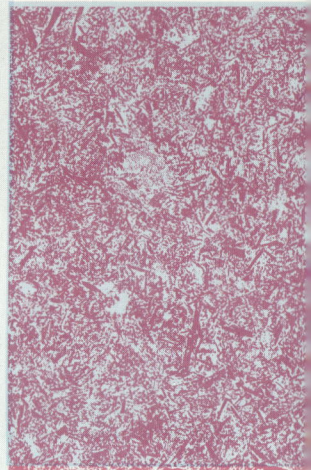

Trying to look as if he belonged there, Peter joined the group of servants who were warming themselves about a fire in the courtyard. And the nightmare began.

"You, too, were with Jesus of Nazareth, the Galilean."

It was the maid who had let him in. "This man was with him," she said to the group around the fire. "Aren't you one of this man's disciples?" she challenged him.

"No," answered Peter.

And as the hours wore on, the nightmare continued: "This is one of them! This man, too, was with Jesus of Nazareth. You, too, are one of them!"

"I don't know the man!"

"Surely you are one of them. Even your speech gives you away as a Galilean. Didn't I see you in the garden with him?"

"I don't know what you're saying. I swear I don't know this man you're speaking about!"

How miserable he felt—like a worm. What a coward he had been! And then Jesus was brought back into the courtyard. He turned toward Peter, and they exchanged a long, meaningful glance. There was no bitterness in Jesus' expression, in spite of Peter's guilt. And that made it even worse. Peter stumbled out of the courtyard, hardly noticing where he was going. He flung himself down somewhere and wept as if his heart would break. The cocks had long since crowed.

Pilate, Roman governor of Judea, was quite undecided that Friday morning. The chief priests had brought him a bruised and bloodstained prisoner, charging that this man was a criminal, a revolutionary who opposed the payment of taxes to Rome and called Himself the Messiah, a king.

Yet when Pilate himself had questioned this Jesus, he had found no evidence against Him. In fact, Jesus had assured him that His kingdom was not of this world. So there was no danger for Rome and nothing to convict the man of. Pilate wanted to let Him go.

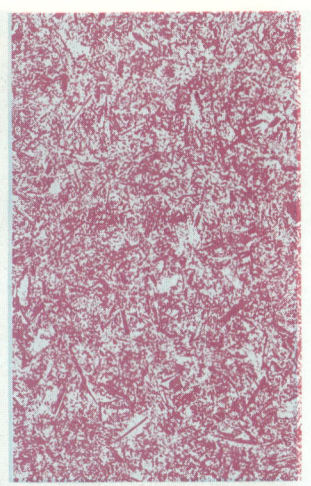

The governor stood on his balcony and gazed down into the angry faces of the chief priests and Pharisees who jammed the narrow street below.

"You have a custom," he reminded them, "of having a Jewish prisoner set free at the Passover. Shall I release Barabbas (a revolutionary and murderer) or Jesus, who is called the Messiah?" He gave them a moment to think it over.

Meanwhile a servant came hurrying out to him with a note. It was from Pilate's wife and it read: "Don't become involved in the case of that good man. I've been greatly disturbed because of a dream about him."

Pilate looked down into that narrow river of faces.

"Which of the two would you like set free?" he repeated.

"Away with this man!" came the cry. "Set Barabbas free!"

Pilate hadn't expected this.

"But what shall I do with Jesus, who is called the Messiah, the King of the Jews?"

"Crucify him!"

"But why? What crime has he committed?"

Then the governor thought of a way of satisfying Jesus' enemies—or at least he **thought** he could satisfy them. "I haven't found any reason for putting him to death, so I'll punish him and let him go."

Did the governor's conscience bother him at that moment? Was it right to punish a man who had done nothing wrong? At any rate, Pilate gave the orders: Jesus was to be scourged (whipped), as convicted criminals usually were before their crucifixion. While the soldiers led Jesus away, Pilate waited a little tensely.

It was some time before they brought Him back. The sight was much worse than Pilate had imagined it would be. So covered with wounds was the prisoner that He hardly seemed to be a human being. And what fiendish idea had gotten into his soldiers—what was this cap of thorns sinking its spines deep into the scourged man's scalp, causing blood to run down His face?

Surely, thought Pilate, this sight would at last move Jesus' enemies to pity. He brought the prisoner forward. "I'm bringing him to you so you may realize that I have found no guilt in him.... Look at the man!"

But Jesus' enemies were determined that He should die, and die at the hands of the Romans so as to be branded a criminal for all time. "Crucify him!" they cried. "Crucify him!"

And then, somehow, the **real** charge came out: "We have a law, and by it he must die because he has called himself God's Son!"

A shiver ran through the governor's whole body. He took Jesus aside and asked, "Where have you come from?"

Until now Jesus had answered Pilate's questions, although He had never defended His innocence. But to **this** question He remained silent. The governor lost his outward calm. "But don't you know that I have the power to set you free and the power to crucify you?" he demanded.

"You wouldn't have any power at all," replied Jesus, "if it were not given to you from above. Therefore the one who has handed me over to you has committed the greater sin."

Again Pilate went out onto the balcony and declared that he would set the prisoner free. But the chief priests knew the governor well—knew what meant the most to him in life.

"If you free this man," someone shouted, "you are no friend of the Emperor!"

Another took up the cry. "Anyone who calls himself king is rebelling against Caesar!"

"Our only king is Caesar!"

They had won, but Pilate felt so strongly about the matter that he called for a basin and washed his hands in the sight of all. "I am innocent of this good man's blood," he declared. Then he ordered that Barabbas be released and Jesus be crucified.

History does not tell us whether the governor slept that night.

John drew nearer to the foot of the cross. He couldn't bear to look into Jesus' pain-twisted face, but neither could he look away. He wanted to support Mary, Jesus' Mother, but he felt so weak himself. It was amazing how Mary could stand so straight there before the cross. The other women who had been allowed to approach Jesus during these last moments were bowed with sorrow and he could hear their muffled sobs.

Through eyes that could hardly see, the Master looked down at His beloved disciple standing beside the person He loved the most on earth. "Woman," He said to Mary, "this is your son."

And then, speaking to John and to **all** His disciples of all ages, He said, "This is your mother."

It had grown extraordinarily dark for early afternoon—dark and cold. Yet Jesus was covered with perspiration as well as with blood. At times His body would sag, His complexion would turn purple and His breathing would become shallow. Great ridges and bulges would stand out all over His body—showing intense cramps in His legs, arms, chest.... Then with a mighty effort He would push Himself higher by straightening His legs. At such moments the ridges of the cramped muscles in the chest would subside, and He could breathe better, but what pain there must have been in His hands and feet!

Yet John had some kind of intuition that by far the worst suffering came from Jesus' vision of the sinfulness and ingratitude of all men of all times.

Jesus' mission was over. He had given the world the noblest set of teachings it would ever hear. He had given it the greatest examples it would ever see. He had given it His very self in the Eucharist. He had suffered for our sins without any inner comfort, so that He actually felt abandoned by His Father. He had given His all. There was nothing left to give.

"It is completed," He said. The world had been redeemed. Jesus bowed His head and died.

Suggested Readings: Mark 14:32-65; Luke 22:54-71; John 18:28—19:42

What do we learn from Jesus' choice of death for our sake?
Jesus' choice of death for our sake teaches us how much He loves us and how terrible sin is.

If you put up with suffering for doing what is right, this is acceptable in God's eyes. It was for this you were called, since Christ suffered for you in just this way and left you an example, to have you follow in his footsteps.

(1 Peter 2:20-21)*

Unit 5
His Saving Mission Continues

22
SUNRISE!

"Peter! John! They've taken away His body! We don't know where He is!"

Mary Magdalene, one of Jesus' most devoted followers, was half sobbing, half gasping for breath. Clearly she had run all the way from the tomb.

The disciples looked at one another. What could this mean? With one accord they set out for Jesus' sepulcher at a dead run.

Although they ran side by side for a while, John gradually outdistanced Peter. He arrived, breathless, at the tomb and peered inside. The wrappings were lying on the ground. Eager as he was to see more, the younger apostle waited for Peter, the leader of the Eleven, and followed him into the chamber where Jesus had lain. Yes, the wrappings were there; the body (which had been placed on a sort of rock shelf) was not. And the piece of cloth that had covered Jesus' head had been neatly rolled up and placed to one side. John felt a spark of hope flaring up within him, but he couldn't express his feelings. In any case, it wasn't safe to stay around making inquiries, because they might be hunted men, as their Leader had been. So the two disciples returned to Jerusalem.

Mary Magdalene had followed them back to the tomb. She was one of those loyal women, such as Jesus' own Mother, John's mother, Joanna and Susanna, who had accompanied Jesus and His disciples on their journeys, listening to His teachings and preparing food for the group. Mary owed much to Jesus. Now the thought that even His **body** had been taken away from them reopened a fresh wound for her. She stood beside the tomb, weeping. As she wept, she looked inside and saw two figures in white. "Why are you crying?" they asked her.

"They have taken the Lord away, and I don't know where they've laid Him."

She turned away again and saw someone else standing near by. "Why are you crying?" another voice asked. "Whom are you looking for?"

Maybe this was the gardener of Joseph of Arimathea, who owned the tomb. "Oh sir," Mary stammered, "if you are the one who carried Him off just tell me where you have laid Him, and I will take Him away!"

"Mary!"

It was **His** voice! It was He—Jesus! "Teacher!"

She flung herself down and embraced His feet.

"Don't cling to me," said Jesus. There were things to be done. "I haven't yet ascended to the Father. Rather, go to my brothers"—and it was the first time He had ever called the apostles His **brothers**—"to tell them 'I am ascending to my Father and your Father, to my God and your God.'"

The sun was bright; the sky was blue. It was spring! The whole world was rejoicing! Mary hurried off to Jerusalem to tell the disciples that Jesus was alive—He had risen!

The disciples were slow to believe Mary Magdalene and the other women who had met Jesus near the tomb that morning. Not until His dramatic appearance that evening did they come to believe. They looked at the marks of His wounds. They watched Him eat and drink. They marveled at His changed appearance and the way He had entered the room through locked doors.

Once they realized that it was truly He, Jesus scolded them for not having believed the women. Only for that did He scold them—not for their desertion of Him the night of His arrest.

And then He told them that they had a mission:

"As the Father has sent me, so I send you."
(John 20:21)*

What happened next reminds us of a line in the book of Genesis:

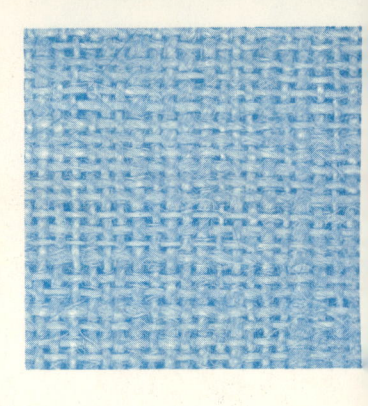

The Lord God formed man...and blew into his nostrils the breath of life, and so man became a living being.

(Genesis 2:17)*

Now Jesus breathed on His apostles and gave them—not natural life—but the Source of "supernatural life"—the Source of grace:

"Receive the Holy Spirit."

(John 20:22)*

And then Jesus, who had died because of the sins of all men, gave us the sacrament by which sins committed after Baptism are forgiven:

*"If you forgive men's sins,
they are forgiven them;
if you hold them bound,
they are held bound."*

(John 20:23)*

The apostles had received the second great power of a priest, the power to forgive sins in Jesus' name.

Thomas, however, had not been present, and he refused to believe the others.

"Unless I can probe the nail marks in His hands and put my hand into His side, I won't believe," Thomas declared.

So Jesus gave him his chance. And it is to Thomas that we owe one of the most beautiful acts of faith to be found in the Gospels:

"My Lord and my God!"

(John 20:28)*

The words Thomas used clearly said, "You are Yahweh; You are God." Jesus had been called "Lord" by His followers before, but apparently it was usually in the sense of "sir." Thomas, instead, plainly stated that Jesus is God, not only the Messiah (Christ, in Greek)—the Lord's Anointed One, sent by Him to save His people—but **God Himself.**

Jesus was very pleased. However, He took the opportunity to teach something to all His followers of all times:

*"You became a believer because
you saw me.
Blest are they who have not seen
and have believed."*

(John 20:29)*

108

In the days that followed, the apostles began to become accustomed to Jesus' absences and sudden appearances. However, there were moments when they simply weren't sure what to do.

One evening they were in Galilee, where Jesus had promised to meet them. Perhaps they had taken the opportunity to put their family and business affairs in order, since they knew they were to continue the work the Savior had begun. In any event, on this particular evening they were there near the Sea of Galilee and Peter announced, "I'm going fishing!"

Peter was a man of action, and time hung heavy on his hands when he didn't have something definite to do.

"We'll come, too," said the others. Peter had always been their leader, next to Jesus, and he still was.

All night long they fished, and caught nothing. At last, just after daybreak, they heard a shout. Someone was standing on the shore. "My friends," the voice called, "have you caught anything?"

"Nothing," they replied.

"Cast the net to starboard."

They did so, and it gathered in so many fish that they couldn't even haul it aboard.

"It's the Lord!" John told Peter. At once Peter put on his cloak and plunged into the water. He half-swam, half-waded ashore. The others followed in the boat, towing the full net, which they had not dared try to lift out of the water.

Jesus already had a small fire blazing. He was cooking their breakfast. Shyly the apostles gathered around Him. The marvelous fact of His resurrection and the wonders of His sudden appearances and disappearances had given them a new reverence for this Man whom they had once treated so familiarly. For in a way not clear to them, this Man was also God.

After the meal, Jesus turned to Peter and asked, "Simon, son of John, do you love me more than these others do?"

Peter was careful in his reply, for he had learned a great lesson during Jesus' passion. At the Last Supper he had been sure enough of himself to declare: "Even if everyone else is shaken in faith, I won't be.... I would lay down my life for You!" He no longer had such trust in himself. But he knew that he loved Jesus very much—so much that the memory of denying Him cut like a sword.

"Yes, Lord," he replied humbly. "You know I love You."

"Feed my lambs," said Jesus.

But then Jesus asked him again, "Simon, son of John, do you love me?"

"Yes, Lord. You know I do."

"Take care of my sheep."

Peter had disowned Jesus at least three distinct times. Now, perhaps without realizing it, he was making reparation (G) for that triple denial.

Jesus asked a third time, "Simon, son of John, do you love me?"

Peter felt hurt. Couldn't Jesus read his heart? "You know everything, Lord. You **know** I love You."

"Feed my sheep," said Jesus.

Jesus had called Himself the Good Shepherd. Now Peter was to be the shepherd in His place—

shepherd of the whole flock that is the Church. He would be in charge of the lambs—the faithful—and the sheep—the other apostles and their successors, the bishops.

He, the first POPE, and each of his successors, would be Jesus' Vicar (the one who would act for Jesus)—the chief teacher and leader of everyone in the Church.

Jesus had also said that the Good Shepherd lays down his life for his sheep. "When you grow old," He told Peter, "you will stretch out your hands and someone will tie you fast." It was an expression that people of that time associated with crucifixion. Peter was to follow Jesus all the way, but his sufferings—and **no** martyr's sufferings—would ever be as intense as those of the Lord. Jesus would give them the spiritual comfort He had not permitted for Himself. His grace would always be sufficient for His faithful ones.

Suggested Readings: John 20:1—21:19

What was the resurrection?
   The resurrection was Jesus' rising from the dead by His divine power.

What did Jesus mean when He said, "As the Father has sent me, so I send you"?
   Jesus meant that the apostles, as leaders of His Church, were to continue His own mission—spreading the Good News of God's saving love.

What is the second great power of a priest?
   The second great power of a priest (after the offering of the Mass) is that of forgiving sins in Jesus' own name in the sacrament of Penance.

What is the Pope's role in the Church?
   The Pope is the Vicar of Christ and the chief teacher and leader of God's people.

"My Lord and my God!"
"...Lord, you know everything; you know that I love you."
(John 20:28; 21:17)**

23 COURAGE FROM THE SPIRIT

At least thirty (perhaps even fifty or fifty-five) years after Jesus' death and resurrection, a book was written to tell us what happened next. For salvation history did not end with Jesus' return to His Father. (As we remember, salvation history is God's loving activity throughout human history to free people from sin and help them to lead good lives so that they will be happy in this life and in the next.)

The death and resurrection of Christ brought a new, spiritual energy into the world—the saving activity of the Holy Spirit, whom Jesus gave to the apostles on Easter and to the whole community of His followers on Pentecost. In fact, through the energy of His Spirit, Jesus is still present in the world today. And He continues to save.

The book called the ACTS OF THE APOSTLES was written by St. Luke and perhaps was originally a continuation of his Gospel. Just as none of the Gospels tells us **everything** about Jesus' life and teachings, so, too, the Acts of the Apostles does not tell us everything about the early life of that community which we now call the Church. Luke was not on the scene at the very beginning. He later interviewed people who knew the facts and gathered whatever written material seemed suitable.

The book's title means "deeds of the apostles." Of all twelve? No; chiefly of Peter, their leader, and Paul, whom Jesus miraculously called a few years after His death and resurrection. Christ singled out Paul for a special mission, as we shall see.

The Acts of the Apostles is sometimes called the "Gospel of the Holy Spirit." One of the first events described in this book is the Spirit's descent upon the group of Jesus' followers, as the Savior had promised. The description of this event (especially the rushing sound of a mighty wind and the leaping flames that descended upon every man and woman in the gathering) recalls various revelations of Yahweh made in Old Testament times.

That particular day was a harvest feast called PENTECOST, which in later Jewish history also recalled the giving of the law on Mount Sinai. From the first Christian Pentecost to our own times, the HOLY SPIRIT has been living in the CHURCH—in the hearts of all its members who do not drive Him out through sin.

Jesus had foretold that the beginning of the Church would be like the planting of a tiny seed:

"The kingdom of heaven is like a mustard seed, which a man took and sowed in his field. It is the smallest of all the seeds, but when it has grown it is the biggest shrub of all and becomes a tree."

(Matthew 13:31-32)**

We might think of the seed as Jesus Himself, who said:

"Unless a wheat grain falls on
 the ground and dies,
it remains only a single grain;
but if it dies,
it yields a rich harvest."

(John 12:24)**

Jesus **died** to give life to His Church. And that life—grace—now joins together people of all different nations and races. They are the new people of God, who were foreshadowed by the chosen people of the Old Testament.

As Jesus had intended, the Church began to function as a community under the headship of the man He had chosen. Guided by the Holy Spirit, Peter acted as leader from the beginning. He called the believers (then, about one hundred twenty) together and asked them to choose another apostle (Matthias) to take Judas' place. On Pentecost He preached the Good News of Jesus. He worked the first miracle that is mentioned in Acts... and the list continues. Peter was definitely the head of Jesus' followers.

Yet this community—which wasn't even called **church** ("assembly") at the beginning—didn't seem independent at first. It started out as if it were another Jewish sect, like the Pharisees, Sadducees, or Essenes. St. Luke gives us these glimpses of the early believers:

They were continually in the Temple praising God.

(Luke 24:53)**

112

They went as a body to the Temple every day.

(Acts 2:46)**

(In their homes, however, they "broke bread"—celebrated the Eucharist.)

St. Luke also tells us that many people were impressed by the miracles worked by the apostles and by their preaching. These people came to believe (through the Holy Spirit's help, for faith is a gift of God), to repent of their sins, and to be baptized. And so the Church grew, right there in Jerusalem.

St. Luke learned, and has passed on to us, some of the incidents of those early days. For example....

It was almost 3:00 P.M.—the afternoon hour for sacrifice in the temple. When on their way to pray, Peter and John passed by a cripple whom some friends had brought to beg at one of the temple gates. Hoping to get something, the beggar called out to the apostles.

Peter stopped and turned toward the man. "Look at us!" he said. The beggar did so.

"I don't have any silver or gold," continued Peter, "but I give you what I have. In the name of Jesus Christ of Nazareth, walk!"

Taking the beggar by the hand, Peter pulled him up. And the man began to walk! In fact, he went on into the temple with Peter and John—walking, jumping around and praising God. Naturally, people turned to see what was going on, and when they recognized the beggar, a whole crowd came swarming over to find out how he had been healed. Peter took advantage of the opportunity to speak about Jesus and repentance.

The beggar, he said, had been healed by God's power because of the apostles' faith in the name of Jesus, "God's Servant." (The "Servant of Yahweh" songs of Second Isaiah had looked ahead to the sufferings of Jesus; for this reason, the apostles often spoke of Jesus as God's Servant.)

Peter reminded his listeners of how good and holy Jesus had been—certainly not deserving to be put to death in place of the murderer Barabbas. And he added:

"God, however, raised him from the dead, and to that fact we are the witnesses....

113

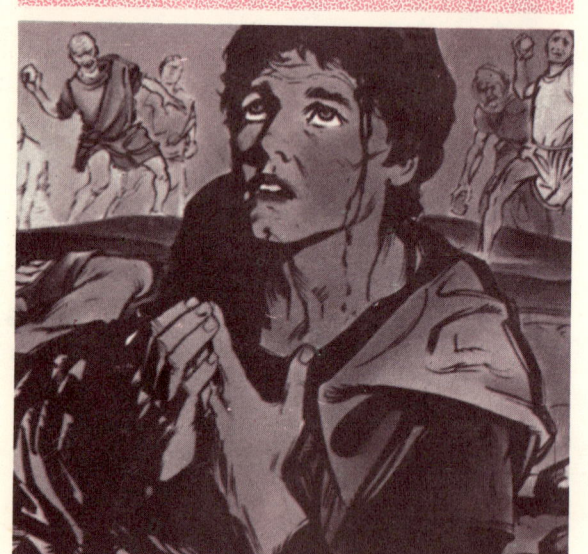

"I know, brothers, that neither you nor your leaders had any idea what you were really doing; this was the way God carried out what he had foretold when he said through all his prophets that his Christ would suffer. Now you must repent and turn to God, so that your sins may be wiped out."

(Acts 3:15, 17-19)**

Peter continued, quoting from the Old Testament, and adding that the resurrection had been first of all for the benefit of the Jewish people, so they might turn to Jesus. Many who listened became believers. Meanwhile, the Sadducees came to break up the gathering. Not believing in the resurrection of the dead at all, they were annoyed by Peter's proclamation of the risen Jesus. They had the captain of the temple police arrest the apostles and take them into custody for the night.

The next day, Peter stood before some of the very men who had brought about Jesus' condemnation to death! But this was a different Peter from the man who had denied his Master at the taunt of a serving girl. When asked to speak, he did so boldly.

The religious leaders were astonished at the apostles' self assurance, especially since they could see that Peter and John were uneducated laymen. They sent them out and began to discuss the situation. What should be done? Perhaps the best thing was to let the whole matter blow over. But the men from Galilee must be forbidden to preach....

They called the apostles back and gave a stern command. Imagine their surprise when Peter and John replied:

"Judge for yourselves whether it is right in God's sight for us to obey you rather than God. Surely we cannot help speaking of what we have heard and seen."

(Acts 4:19-20)*

There was nothing the leaders could do. After all, the whole city was praising God for the cure of that beggar, who had been crippled ever since his birth forty-some-odd years before! So they let the apostles go.

But persecution (G) couldn't be avoided forever. One day, perhaps six years after Jesus' ascension (G), a deacon (G) named Stephen was charged with putting Jesus above the temple and the law of Moses. During his trial Stephen so clearly accused the religious leaders of having had Jesus killed that they pounced on him in a mob, dragged him out of the city and stoned him to death.

A young Pharisee named Saul, who had approved of Stephen's death, felt that the teachings of this "new way" were dangerous. Determined to stamp out the new faith, he began to arrest and imprison Jesus' followers and to press for their death. He followed them far and wide, for because of his persecution they soon scattered throughout Judea and Samaria and even to distant cities.

Jesus' followers did not go into **hiding,** however. Wherever they went, they began to tell their Jewish brothers and sisters that the Messiah had come. And the number of believers continued to grow.

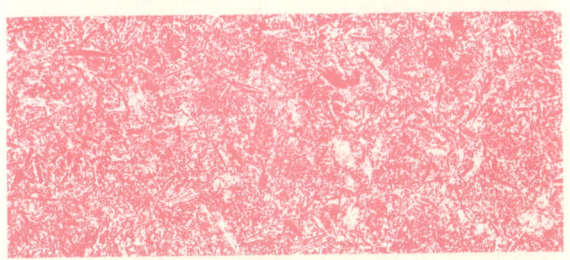

Suggested Readings: Acts, chapters 1–5 and 7:54–8:8

Did salvation history end with the death and resurrection of Jesus?

Salvation history did not end with Jesus' death and resurrection. Through the work of the Holy Spirit, Jesus still acts to save in our world today.

What do we mean by the Acts of the Apostles?

The Acts of the Apostles is the book of the Bible that tells us much about the growth of the early Church, guided by the Holy Spirit. The chief personalities in this book are the apostles Peter and Paul.

Where and how did the Church begin?

The Church began in Jerusalem with the death of Jesus and His sending of the Spirit. Working through the miracles and preaching of the apostles, the Holy Spirit drew many of Jesus' countrymen into the new community of believers.

Give thanks to the Lord, for he is good,
  for his mercy endures forever.
The stone which the builders rejected
  has become the cornerstone.
By the Lord has this been done;
  it is wonderful in our eyes.

This is the day the Lord has made;
  let us be glad and rejoice in it.
              (Psalm 118:1, 22-24)*

24
THE THIRTEENTH APOSTLE

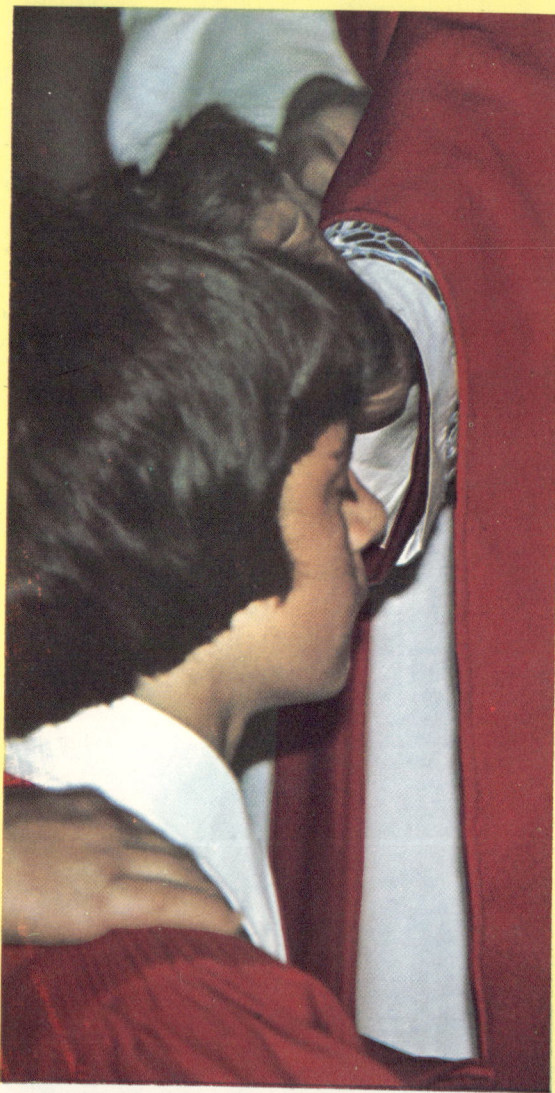

As we have seen, persecution actually made the "new way" spread from Jerusalem to other towns and cities.

A deacon named Philip even began to preach in a Samaritan town. The Samaritans believed in one God as the Jews did, and they, too, had been waiting for the Messiah.

Philip's preaching, like that of the apostles and Stephen, was accompanied by miracles, such as cures of paralytics and cripples. Many came to believe and be baptized. Belief, repentance and Baptism were the entrance-way into the new faith.

Philip sent word to the apostles who had remained in Jerusalem in spite of the persecution. Soon Peter and John came to Samaria and accepted the Samaritans as members of the Church (although actually the words "Church" and "Christian" had not come into use yet).

Peter and John also **confirmed** the men and women whom Philip had baptized. This reminds us of an important point: a deacon—or **anyone**, when it is necessary—can baptize; Confirmation, instead, is given by a bishop or by a priest with the bishop's permission. The apostles were the first bishops.

As we have mentioned already, BAPTISM and CONFIRMATION are sacraments—the chief ways in which Jesus gives us His Spirit to make us holy by grace. We are not sure just **when** Jesus gave His Church the sacrament of Confirmation, but from this passage in Acts and also from another one we can see that He **did** establish this sacrament.

Perhaps Jesus made Baptism a sacrament not long before His ascension. St. Mark tells us:

> He said to them, "Go out to the whole world; proclaim the Good News to all creation. He who believes and is baptized will be saved."
> (Mark 16:16)**

The Gospels tell us that Jesus instituted (established) the sacraments of HOLY EUCHARIST and HOLY ORDERS at the Last Supper and the sacrament of PENANCE on the very day of His resurrection.

We do not know **when** our Savior instituted the ANOINTING OF THE SICK, but we do know **that** He did, because of Divine Tradition (G) and the Church's administration of the sacrament down through the centuries. In addition, a book of the New Testament called the Letter (Epistle) of James says:

> If one of you is ill, he should send for the elders of the church, and they must anoint him with oil in the name of the Lord and pray over him. The prayer of faith will save the sick man and the Lord will raise him up again; and if he has committed any sins, he will be forgiven.
> (James 5:14-15)**

The remaining sacrament is MATRIMONY. And from Tradition and the teaching of the Spirit-guided Church we know that it, too, is a sacrament. Several passages in the New Testament tell us that marriage is holy and only to be broken by death.

The sacraments are the means Jesus gave us for staying close to Him. When our Savior taught His followers what we are to believe and do in order to be saved (set free from sin and brought to God), He was asking much of them, and of us. But with the help of the sacraments we can do what He asks! In fact, at times it even becomes easy. Through the sacraments our Savior gives us spiritual strength and energy.

The sacraments are one of our great treasures. They were given to the Church at the cost of Jesus' passion and death. The Shepherd died to give life to His sheep. It is through the sacraments that the Church brings people the salvation (G) that Jesus won for them.

The persecution in Judea had driven some of Jesus' followers as far as Damascus, where they probably took refuge among relatives and acquaintances already living there. (For centuries there had been Jewish communities in many leading cities of the Near East and Mediterranean world.)

SAUL followed the refugees, determined to bring them back to Jerusalem under arrest. All the while, of course, he really thought he was serving God. Jesus had foretold this situation:

> "Indeed the hour is coming when anyone who kills you will think he is doing a holy duty for God."
> (John 16:2)**

Jesus Himself was waiting for Saul on that road to Damascus. It was around the year 36 A.D. (Probably the Savior had made His last appearance to His apostles about six years before.) We know what happened, for Saul himself later told about it:

> "As I was traveling along, approaching Damascus around noon, a great light from the sky suddenly flashed all about me. I fell to the ground and heard a voice say to me, 'Saul, Saul, why do you persecute me?' I answered, 'Who are you, sir?' He said to me, 'I am Jesus the Nazorean, whom you are persecuting.' '...What is it I must do, sir?' I asked."
> (Acts 22:6-8, 10)*

What an amazing readiness to do God's will! Surely the Lord must have been preparing Saul for this moment. In fact, Saul would later write:

The time came when he who had set me apart before I was born and called me by his favor chose to reveal his Son to me.
(Galatians 1:15-16)*

Saul was to have a special mission. As Jesus directed, he went into Damascus, where one of the Lord's followers baptized him. Then he set out into Arabia—probably the region southeast of Damascus—to pray and learn what God wanted of him. He was taught directly by Jesus, whom more than once he saw in a vision, as we are told in several passages of Scripture, such as these:

"The Lord answered: '...I have appeared to you for this reason: to appoint you as my servant and as witness of this vision in which you have seen me, and of others in which I shall appear to you.'"
(Acts 26:15-16)**

I am an apostle and I have seen Jesus our Lord.
(1 Corinthians 9:1)**

Brothers, the gospel I proclaimed to you...came by revelation from Jesus Christ.
(Galatians 1:11-12)*

It seems that Saul stayed in the desert only a few months. Then he returned to Damascus and spent three years there, teaching his countrymen that Jesus was the Messiah. Of course, everyone was amazed that the persecutor of the "new way" had turned about and joined it! But Saul spoke with such sureness that some of his listeners, too, became followers of Jesus.

The new apostle also made enemies, who plotted to have him arrested. So one night, by means of ropes, his disciples lowered him from the city wall in a large basket or hamper, such as traders used. For this determined preacher of the Good News, this was to be the first of many such escapes.

The natural place to go to was Jerusalem. How did the disciples there receive him? With fear and distrust. Of course, Saul really couldn't blame them, but he must have felt quite uncomfortable until a kind and generous disciple named BARNABAS took him around and introduced him, explaining that Saul truly had seen and talked with Jesus. Then they accepted him.

The former persecutor even spent some time with Peter and Jesus' cousin, James, before he left for Tarsus, the city in Asia Minor (modern Turkey) where his own family lived. There Saul prayed, worked (probably making tents—the trade he usually followed to support himself) and doubtless preached, while he waited for a sign of what God wanted him to do next.

After Saul's conversion, the persecution died down. During this new period of peace, Peter went about in Judea, visiting the various communities of Jesus' followers that had sprung up. While staying at Joppa, where he brought a dead woman back to life by God's power, he was granted an important vision.

He was praying on the roof terrace of the house where he was staying. It was about noon, and he grew hungry. Then a trance came over him. He saw something that looked like a big canvas come down out of the sky, lowered by its four corners. It came to rest in front of him and he could see that it was full of all sorts of animals. "Stand up, Peter," a voice said. "Kill and eat."

Many of the animals belonged to the "unclean" category, according to the ancient laws God had given His people. "Sir," protested Peter, "I wouldn't dream of it! I've never eaten anything unclean!"

The voice replied, "What God has made clean you must not call unclean."

Three times this happened. Then the object disappeared into the sky. At the same time, the Holy Spirit inspired Peter, "Two men have just arrived. They're downstairs looking for you. Go with them without hesitation, for it is I who sent them."

Peter went downstairs and met the men, who told him, "We have come from Cornelius the centurion, who was instructed by a heavenly messenger to invite you to his home in Caesarea. He is a good man, who has reverence for God and is respected by the whole Jewish community. He wishes to hear what you have to say."

"Come in," said Peter. He was beginning to understand the meaning of his vision.

These men who had come to him were non-Jews—also called GENTILES. It was clear from the way Cornelius had been described that the centurion himself was also a Gentile. (Non-Jews were often accepted into the Jewish religion, but only if they fulfilled a number of required conditions. Others, who only accepted belief in the one God and attended services in the local synagogue, were called God-fearers. Cornelius must have been one of these.)

Jews would not eat with Gentiles. This was partly due to the laws about clean and unclean food. Now Peter saw that the Spirit wanted him to treat these men on an equal footing. So the messengers stayed with him overnight, and the next morning he set out for Caesarea with them, accompanied by six disciples from Joppa.

Cornelius was waiting for them. In fact, he had invited his relatives and close friends to come and hear Peter's words. Without hesitation, the apostle entered the Gentile's house, where Cornelius informed him of an angelic apparition (G) in which he had been told to send for Peter.

So Peter began to preach the Good News of Jesus.

The fact that the heavenly messenger hadn't delivered the Lord's saving message himself but had told Cornelius to send for Peter shows us that God prefers to work through men rather than directly or through angels. Incidents like the conversion and instruction of Saul have always been exceptional events in salvation history. God usually works in more ordinary, less spectacular ways.

As Peter spoke, the whole gathering of Gentiles began to praise the Lord, just as the Pentecost community had done. Clearly, the Holy Spirit had come upon them. Seeing that God Himself made no distinction between Jew and Gentile, Peter asked his companions from Joppa to baptize the group. And then he stayed with the Gentiles a few days, at their request.

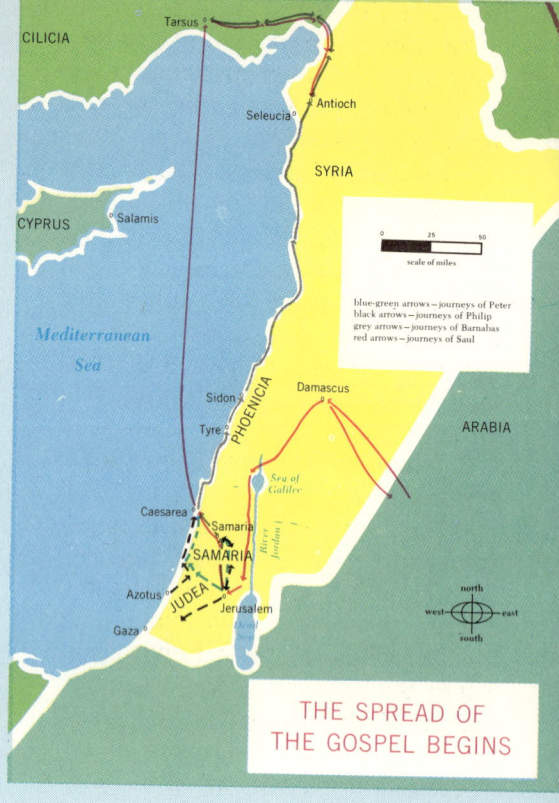

The words of Jesus before His ascension were beginning to be carried out:

"Go, therefore, make disciples of all the nations."

(Matthew 28:19)**

THE SPREAD OF THE GOSPEL BEGINS

Suggested Readings: Acts 9:1-31; 10:1-48; 12:1-18; Matthew 28:16-20; Mark 16:15-20

How far back in history can the sacraments be traced?

Through Scripture and Tradition the Church can trace the sacraments back to Jesus and the very beginnings of Christianity.

What were the names of the apostles?

The first eleven were: Peter, John, James, Andrew, Philip, Thomas, Bartholomew, Matthew, James, Simon, and Jude Thaddeus. Matthias was added to replace Judas, and Paul received a special call from Jesus a few years after His ascension.

Blessed be God the Father of our Lord Jesus Christ, who in his great mercy has given us a new birth as his sons.

(1 Peter 1:3)**

25 A GREAT RUNNER — A GREAT RACE

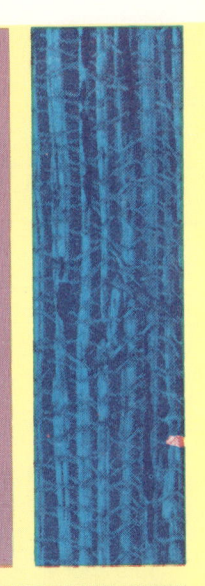

By this time, the "new way" had spread to towns and cities of Judea, Samaria and Galilee, as well as to Jewish communities in Cyprus and Phoenicia. In the Syrian city of ANTIOCH, some of Jesus' followers began to preach the Good News to the Gentiles, too, and brought them into their community. When the believers in Jerusalem heard of this, they sent Barnabas to see the situation firsthand. This was around 44 A.D.

Barnabas was pleased with what he saw. Here were Jewish and Gentile believers worshiping together in one community. Certainly this was God's own doing — this was what He wanted. And it seemed that still more Gentiles were interested in this new way of belief and of life.

Antioch was not far from Tarsus, birthplace of Saul. Knowing that this enthusiastic apostle would be eager to preach the Good News in the new community, Barnabas sought him out and brought him back to Antioch. There both of them began to instruct great numbers of converts. (Perhaps among them was St. Luke, who is thought to have come from Antioch.) It was here that Jesus' followers were first called CHRISTIANS — disciples of Christ.

One day, when the Christian community of Antioch was at prayer, the Holy Spirit enlightened them to send Barnabas and Saul on a missionary journey. At last the time had come! It was about 45 A.D., perhaps fifteen years after Jesus' death, resurrection and ascension.

Barnabas and PAUL (for in the Gentile world Saul would use a Greek name) started out by sailing to Cyprus, Barnabas' place of origin. After preaching there and making converts, they voyaged on to Perga on the coast of Asia Minor and then continued inland on foot to another Antioch, located in the Roman province of Pisidia. Continuing on to Iconium, Lystra, Derbe and the surrounding country, they preached to the Jews and Gentiles of each place.

The following incident — which took place at Lystra — shows us what the apostles were up against. While Paul was preaching to the Gentiles, he saw

ST PAUL'S FIRST MISSIONARY JOURNEY

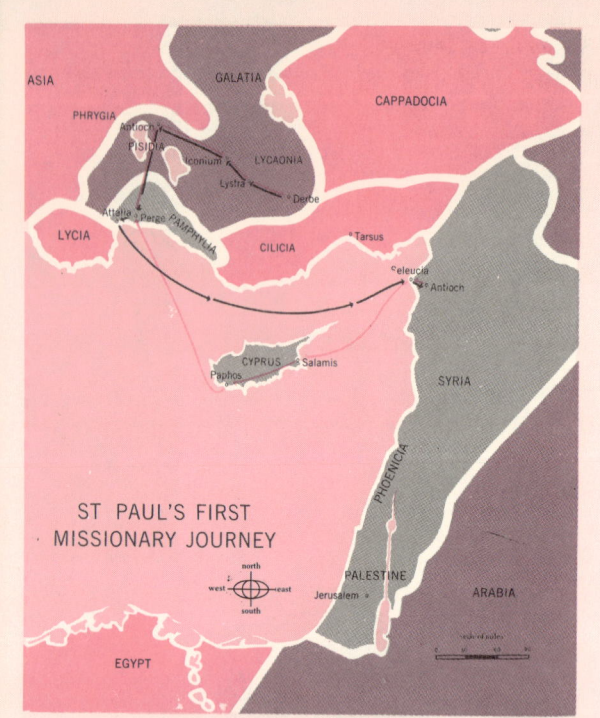

a cripple listening intently. "Stand up!" the apostle called out. At once the man jumped up and began to walk. But what did the Gentiles think? "Zeus (G) and Hermes (G) have come to us in the form of men!" they shouted. Instead of praising the one, true God, they bowed to the ground before the two missionaries. In fact, they even called a pagan priest to sacrifice oxen to Paul and Barnabas.

"Friends!" shouted Paul above the clamor of the crowd. "We're only men like yourselves. We've come here to bring the Good News that will convert you to the living God from just such foolishness as this." But it was hard to bring the people to understand.

Persecutions also took place. Again in Lystra, Paul was stoned by a mob and dragged out of the town. But as his new disciples crowded around him, thinking that he was dead, he stood up, dusted himself off, and went back into the town.

This was typical of Paul. He was all for Jesus and the spreading of the Good News, no matter what the cost to himself. (He could never forget what he had done to Jesus in persecuting His followers.) And because he was all for Jesus, Jesus was all for him, helping him so much that Paul once wrote:

> In him who is the source of my strength I have strength for everything.
>
> (Philippians 4:13)*

From Derbe the missionaries retraced their steps to the coast. In each city that they had evangelized, they installed "presbyters," Church officials who seem to have been similar to today's priests. Then they sailed back to Syrian Antioch, their starting point. The journey had taken about three years.

Not long after the missionaries' return to Antioch, a delegation came from Judea to tell the Gentile believers that in order to be Christians it was necessary to first become Jews. This brought about a meeting which settled the difficulty. Paul and Barnabas went to Jerusalem to consult with Peter, John, Jesus' cousin James, and other leaders of the Christian community. This assembly, which probably took place in 49 A.D., is sometimes called the COUNCIL of Jerusalem. Peter and other leaders decided that the Gentiles who wanted to become Christians did not have to follow the whole Jewish law. (Of course, Christians **do** have to live by the part of the law of Moses that we call the ten commandments. **All** people have to do this. As we know, our Savior even made these commandments more complete and perfect, so that Christians—the new people of God—could live holier lives and grow closer to Him.)

Eager to visit the Christian communities that he and Barnabas had established, Paul set out from Antioch —perhaps toward the end of 49 A.D. with Silas, one of the Jerusalem Church's leading prophets. (Yes, the New-Testament era had its prophets, too!) They traveled through various Roman provinces in Asia Minor, encouraging the Christian communities at Derbe, Lystra and Iconium, which Paul had founded with Barnabas.

At Lystra, Paul and Silas were joined by a young man named TIMOTHY, who was to become as dear to Paul as a son.

They continued on through Asia Minor, preaching the Good News to both Jews and Gentiles. By God's providence, Jewish communities existed throughout the Roman Empire. This scattering of communities had begun at the time of the Exile. It was called the DIASPORA, or "dispersion," which simply means scattering. Loyal to Yahweh, these Jewish people had brought the knowledge of the one, true God among the Gentiles. Now Paul and his companions came to explain that Yahweh had sent the Messiah, who had died for the sake of all men and wished to form mankind into one, holy people—a people that soon came to be called the CHURCH (assembly or gathering).

The Good News caught on. More Christian communities sprang up in Asia Minor. Then, at Troas on the Aegean Sea, Paul had a vision in which a man invited him, "Come over to Macedonia and help us."

Macedonia lay in what today we would call northern Greece. As far as we know, it was the first part of Europe in which the Good News was preached.

The chief cities in which the missionaries established Christian communities were Philippi, Thessalonica and Beroea. But first, in Philippi, Paul and Silas were arrested, scourged and imprisoned for disturbing the peace! Of course, there was no basis for the charges. The next day the city officials sent word to set them free. Meanwhile, however, the missionaries had been miraculously released from prison and had converted the jailer, together with his whole household!

ST PAUL'S SECOND MISSIONARY JOURNEY

In the province of Achaia (which today we would call southern Greece), Paul made a few converts in the intellectual city of Athens and many more in the bustling commercial center of Corinth. He stayed in Corinth a year and a half, supporting himself by making tents. Paul was a great worker. During this time (around 51 A.D.) he also wrote what were probably the first books of the New Testament to be written. (As we remember, the **Gospels** were set down later—between 60 and 100 A.D.) These books of Paul's were "epistles," or letters, called 1 and 2 THESSALONIANS.

Persecution had forced Paul into leaving Thessalonica hurriedly, and now he wrote to the new Christians there, praising their steadfastness in persecution. He also gave some practical advice and tried to lead them to a better understanding of the "parousia"—Jesus' second coming at the end of the world.

Paul wrote in Greek, and we might stop to think about why this was important. Divine providence seems to have been at work in making Greek such a key language in the first-century world. You see, the Greeks had just the **right word** for everything. With all the new and marvelous realities which Jesus' followers wanted to tell others about— such as the Savior's divinity (G), the divine life within us that we call grace, the selfless love that Christians should have for one another—they needed a very clear and exact language. In Greek they had this.

The whole New Testament was written in Greek, even though certain portions of it seem to have first been set down in Aramaic, the common language of the Jewish people at that time.

Now, of course, we have English translations, and these, too, are very important, for the Bible was written just as much for **us** as for the people of biblical times.

124

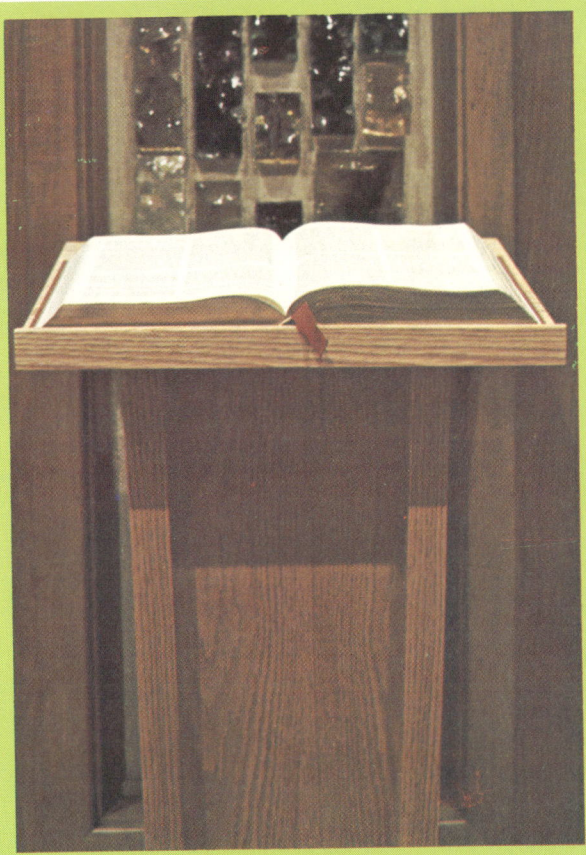

Paul's second missionary journey ended with his return to Jerusalem and Antioch, by way of Ephesus, a seaport in Asia Minor. The year was about 52 A.D., and in 53 or 54 he was on the move again.

The third journey took Paul through the heart of Asia Minor and back to Ephesus, where he spent at least two and a half years. It was probably during this time that he wrote to the Christian communities of Galatia, a province of central Asia Minor through which he had passed more than once on his journeys. GALATIANS treats the question of Gentiles becoming Jews before becoming Christians. It tells about the freedom of Christians, a freedom which is always to be used in good ways, in obedience to God's commandments.

The letter also tells us much about Paul and contains some famous lines, such as this one:

The life I live now is not my own; Christ is living in me.
(Galatians 2:20)*

This shows how close to Jesus a person becomes when he or she is concerned only about serving the Lord.

It seems that Paul was imprisoned at one point during his stay in Ephesus (perhaps in 56 or 57 A.D.) and that while a prisoner he received a gift of financial help from the Christian community he had founded in Philippi. This was at least the third time that these disciples had done this for him, and he wrote PHILIPPIANS to thank them. Besides showing Paul's great affection, this letter contains a beautiful poem (Phil. 2:5-11) which —whether written by him or only quoted by him—clearly shows the early Church's firm belief that Jesus is God.

125

During Paul's stay in Ephesus (around Easter in the year 57), a delegation arrived from Corinth to ask him certain questions that were troubling the Corinthians. His reply was the letter which we call 1 CORINTHIANS. (Actually, it was not really his first letter to the community at Corinth; the first has been lost.) Many of the problems treated in this letter are like those of our own times.

In his letters (for example, in 1 Corinthians 9:23-27) Paul liked to compare his life to a race. He was running to win the prize—heaven—a much greater prize, he said, than any earthly championship.

The apostle was running in another race, too—a race against time. There were so many people he wanted to bring to Christ before he died! How precious time was to him! He was careful never to lose a moment.

It seems that the troubles of the Corinthians grew worse, causing Paul to pay them a quick visit, which he followed up with another letter. (This letter, too, has been lost.) Then, probably in the autumn of that same year, while Paul was returning to Corinth by way of Macedonia, he wrote what we call 2 CORINTHIANS. In this letter he showed what an affectionate heart he had and how deeply he had been hurt by opposition from members of the Corinthian community. He also left us a sketch of what he had already gone through for love of Christ:

Five times...I received forty lashes less one; three times I was beaten with rods; I was stoned once, shipwrecked three times; I passed a day and a night on the sea. I traveled continually, endangered by floods, robbers, my own people, the Gentiles; imperiled in the city, in the desert, at sea, by false brothers; enduring labor, hardship, many sleepless nights; in hunger and thirst and frequent fastings, in cold and nakedness. Leaving other sufferings unmentioned, there is that daily tension pressing on me, my anxiety for all the churches....
(2 Corinthians 11:24-28)*

It was probably from Corinth, early in the year 58, that Paul wrote the famous letter called ROMANS, which stresses the importance of the Good News, grace and the Christian life. Romans also shows that God's plan for our salvation through Christ does not contradict the promises that He made to Israel.

From Achaia Paul and several companions returned to Jerusalem, traveling overland through Macedonia and then by boat across the Aegean and Mediterranean. They brought with them a collection that the Christians of Galatia, Macedonia and Achaia had taken up for their poorer fellow-Christians in Jerusalem. The poor have always been a great concern of the Church.

ST. PAUL'S THIRD MISSIONARY JOURNEY

On the way to Jerusalem, they met a prophet who said that Paul would be taken prisoner. Hearing this, Luke and Paul's other companions tried to persuade him to turn back. But this is what he replied:

"Why are you crying and breaking my heart in this way? For the name of the Lord Jesus I am prepared, not only for imprisonment, but for death, in Jerusalem."

(Acts 21:13)*

Suggested Readings: Acts 13:1-12; 14:8-23; 16:16-40; Romans 12:9-18; 1 Corinthians 13:1-13

Where did the name "Christian" originate?

The name Christian—which comes from "Christ," the Greek word for Messiah—was first given to Jesus' followers in Antioch.

What does "Church" mean?

Church means gathering or assembly.

What difficulty did the Council of Jerusalem clear up?

The Council of Jerusalem declared that it was not necessary for Gentiles to follow the whole Jewish law in order to enter the Church.

Blessed be God the Father of our Lord Jesus Christ,
who has blessed us with all the spiritual blessings of heaven in Christ.
Before the world was made, he chose us, chose us in Christ,
to be holy and spotless, and to live through love in his presence,
determining that we should become his adopted sons, through Jesus Christ
for his own kind purposes,
to make us praise the glory of his grace,
his free gift to us in the Beloved,
in whom, through his blood, we gain our freedom, the forgiveness of our sins.

(Ephesians 1:3-7)**

127

26
TO THE ENDS OF THE EARTH

ST. PAUL'S FOURTH MISSIONARY JOURNEY

"Throw some of the cargo overboard!"

A fierce wind screamed through the ship's rigging. Giant waves crashed against its hull. The Rome-bound vessel was caught in the grip of a northeaster.

Paul and his two companions—Luke and Aristarchus—watched the seamen pass the precious cargo up from the hold and drop it into the sea to lighten the ship. Would this effort keep the towering waves from swamping the vessel?

Winter was the wrong time of year for sailing; in fact, the captain and crew had intended to stop over in a port on the southern coast of Crete, but in the meantime this storm had caught them and driven them far from land. It looked as though they might well be lost—shipowner, captain, seamen, soldiers and prisoners.

One of the prisoners was Paul. Incorrectly accused of bringing Gentiles into the temple, he had been rescued from a lynch mob and taken into custody by Roman soldiers. Now he was on his way to Rome to set his case before the emperor, Nero. Along with the other prisoners on board, he had been placed in the care of a kindly centurion named Julius.

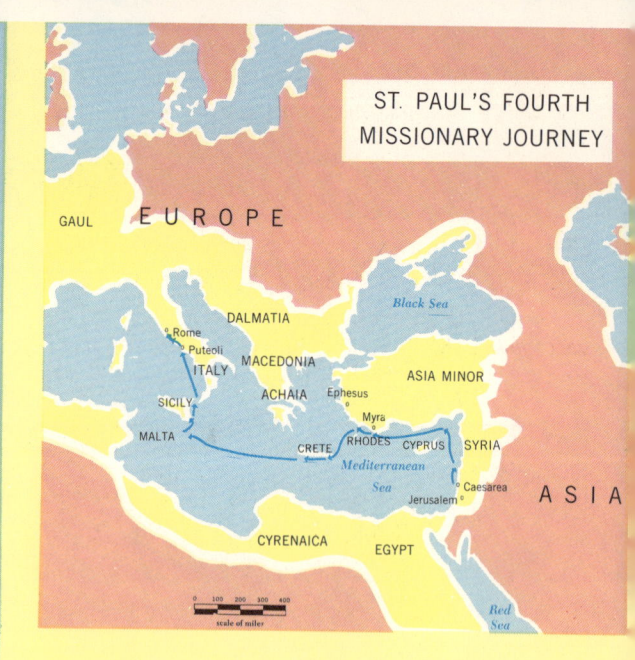

Days passed with no glimpse of sun or stars. Just at the point when everyone was giving up hope, Paul announced, "Don't despair. No one's life will be lost—only the ship. Last night a messenger of the God whom I belong to and serve stood beside me and said, 'Don't be afraid, Paul. You are to appear before the emperor. Because of this God has granted safety to everyone who is sailing with you.'"

In the middle of the fourteenth night, the seamen sensed that land was near. Sure enough! Shortly after dawn they ran firmly aground on a sand bar.

"All who can swim, into the sea!" ordered Julius, the centurion. "Everyone else, follow on planks and pieces of wreckage." (The pounding waves were fast breaking up the ship's stern.)

Following these directives, everyone came safely to land.

Friendly natives of the island (Malta) welcomed them and helped them build a fire on the beach so they could dry out. Paul collected some brushwood. As he was feeding the fire with it, a poisonous snake came gliding out of nowhere and fastened itself on the apostle's hand.

The natives gasped and murmured, "What a criminal this man must be if Justice is taking his life after he escaped from the sea!" Yet Paul simply shook the snake off into the flames as if nothing had happened. After watching him for some time, the natives decided that instead of a criminal he must be a god, for the poisonous bite hadn't harmed him at all.

The shipwreck-victims spent the rest of the winter on Malta, during which time Paul cured all the sick of the island who were brought to him.

The following spring Paul and his shipmates boarded a vessel bound for Italy, where they were greeted by Christians from two cities, Puteoli and Rome. Guarded by a soldier, Paul spent the next two years in a room he rented. Visitors were freely allowed to come and go, so he was able to continue his mission of preaching and instructing.

This is where the Acts of the Apostles ends — with Paul in Rome awaiting trial. Why did Luke end his account there? No one can be sure, but perhaps it was because Paul had now reached the center of the Empire; in other words, another stage in the spread of Christianity had been completed. With Rome as its center, the Christian Faith was next to radiate "to the ends of the earth," as Jesus had commanded (see Acts 1:8), and Luke may have decided to leave **that** story to historians of future centuries.

During this period of captivity in Rome (about 61-63 A.D.), Paul seems to have written three letters, which are called the epistles to the COLOSSIANS, to the EPHESIANS and to PHILEMON.

A problem had arisen in the belief of the Christian community at Colossae (in Asia Minor). It seems that some believers thought the angels more important than Jesus. In COLOSSIANS, Paul emphasizes the fact that Jesus is God.

The letter called EPHESIANS was probably meant for all the Christian communities in the region of Ephesus and Colossae. It treats the Church, Jesus' mystical body (G).

As usual, both of these letters also give practical advice about how to lead a good Christian life.

PHILEMON is a letter to a friend of Paul's at Colossae. Paul tells his friend that Philemon's runaway slave is coming back to him, sorry for what he has done. The apostle asks Philemon to welcome the slave with Christian goodness, "as a brother."

From various sources, we know that Paul was set free around 62 or 63

A.D. We are not sure where he went then. Perhaps he sailed to Spain, as he had hoped to do. He also revisited the lands of the eastern Mediterranean.

While there, he wrote to two of his disciples, Timothy and Titus, who were in charge of the Christian communities at Ephesus and Crete. 1 TIMOTHY and TITUS contain instructions about how to govern the Church well. From these letters we can see that the system the Church has had through the centuries — dioceses governed by bishops with priests and deacons as their helpers — was already beginning to take shape. This organization resembled the very effective system of governing that the Romans used.

In the summer of 64 A.D., the first Roman persecution broke out. As had happened to Jesus before them, the Christians were accused of what they had not done.

At some point after that, Paul was again taken prisoner. While awaiting trial, he wrote 2 TIMOTHY, which might be considered his last will and testament. In this letter he encouraged his "son in the faith" to live as a good Christian and leader in the Church. Then he added:

The time has come for me to be gone. I have fought the good fight to the end; I have run the race to the finish; I have kept the faith.
(2 Timothy 4:6-7)**

From now on a merited crown awaits me; on that Day the Lord, just judge that he is, will award it to me....
(2 Timothy 4:8)*

Yes, Paul's great race had ended. ROME was its finish line. Probably sometime in the year 67 A.D. he was taken to a place outside the city walls and put to death by the sword for his Christian belief. Visitors to Rome may see the place of his martyrdom, the Three Fountains, with its neighboring tiny prison cell where the apostle spent his last night on earth.

Peter, too, had made his way to Rome. In fact, he was in direct charge of the Roman Christians — in other words, he was Rome's bishop. Around the time Paul was imprisoned — or perhaps even before then — Peter, too, was seized by the Roman authorities and condemned to death. They took him to a hill called the Vatican to crucify him.

Peter looked at the cross, so like the one on which Jesus had died. He didn't feel worthy to suffer the same kind of death. "Crucify me upside down," he requested. So they did.

Peter had come a long way since Good Friday.

Today St. Peter's Basilica (G) stands on that same hill. And deep beneath it lie the bones of the first Pope. Ever since Peter's time, the BISHOP OF ROME has been the visible leader of the Church — the Pope, the Holy Father, the Vicar of Christ.

And ever since then, Peter and Paul — the first Pope and the apostle who brought more people to Jesus than any other — have been special protectors of the Church.

God's saving love for the world continued to show itself through the lives of the early Christians, who amazed the pagans by their goodness at all times and their courage during persecution. Without God's loving help, they never could have done what they did. Already they were experiencing the truth of Jesus' words:

"Know that I am with you always, until the end of the world!"
(Matthew 28:20)*

His love also showed itself through the rest of New Testament revelation, namely:

HEBREWS—a letter that was probably written by one of Paul's disciples, since it seems to have been influenced by Paul's thinking. Hebrews may have been written around 67 A.D. It encourages persecuted Jewish Christians, urging them to stay loyal to Christ, our High Priest.

JAMES—a letter that is a sort of sermon on the Christian life. It may have been written sometime before 62 A.D. by James, "the brother (cousin) of the Lord."

JUDE—a letter written against persons who were spreading false teachings. It may have been written between 70 and 80 A.D. by the brother of that James who was just mentioned.

1 PETER—a practical letter which has the theme of patience in difficulty and persecution. It was probably written by Peter and/or a disciple of his at Rome in the early 60's.

2 PETER—a letter that may have been written around the end of the first century to warn against false teachings. Perhaps the author was one of Peter's disciples. (Using another person's name was common and acceptable in those days.)

1, 2 and 3 JOHN—three letters written by John, the apostle and evangelist (Gospel-writer). They were probably written around the end of the first century (in the 90's). The first of the three is the most important. One of its main themes is love for God and others because God has so loved us.

The Book of REVELATION is not a letter. It belongs to a type of writing called apocalyptic, which means that it uses symbols to describe a great struggle between good and evil. Scripture experts tell us that much of the symbolism in Revelation can be understood by a person who is familiar

131

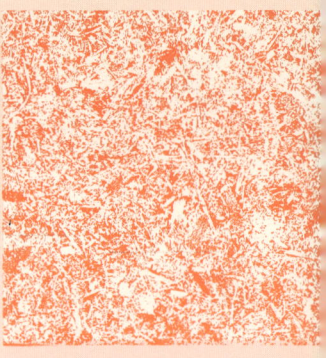

with such Old Testament books as Ezekiel, Daniel, Isaiah and Zechariah. The Book of Revelation assures us of the final victory of Christ and His followers over the powers of evil. It was written by St. John and/or his disciples for the purpose of encouraging persecuted Christians. The time of writing may have been between 70 and 95 A.D.

John was the apostle who lived the longest. With his death came the end of the special REVELATION that God had been giving to mankind through SCRIPTURE and TRADITION. The Church no longer needed to receive new teachings from God. Rather, under the Holy Spirit's guidance it was to deepen its understanding of what God had already communicated to mankind through the Bible and Tradition.

Yet SALVATION HISTORY did not end with the completion of revelation. Through God's Word (the Bible), through the Mass and sacraments, through the teachings of the Church, the Father, Son and Holy Spirit continue to come into our lives. Now, as always, they act to **save** us—to free us from sin and lead us to everlasting happiness.

The plan of the Lord stands forever.
(Psalm 33:11)*

Suggested Readings: Acts 27:1 – 28:10; James 2:14-17; 1 John 4:7-16

How may the New Testament be divided?
We may divide the New Testament into historical books (the Gospels and Acts), instructional books (twenty-one epistles or letters), and one apocalyptic book.

In what ways does God continue to act to save us?
God acts to save us through the Mass and sacraments, through the Bible, through the teachings of the Church and in other ways.

At Jesus' name
every knee must bend
in the heavens, on the earth,
and under the earth,
and every tongue proclaim
to the glory of God the Father:
JESUS CHRIST IS LORD!
(Philippians 2:10-11)*

GUIDELINES FOR CHRISTIAN LIVING

THE TEN COMMANDMENTS OF GOD

1. I, the Lord, am your God. You shall not have other gods besides me.
2. You shall not take the name of the Lord, your God, in vain.
3. Remember to keep holy the Lord's day.
4. Honor your father and your mother.
5. You shall not kill.
6. You shall not commit adultery.
7. You shall not steal.
8. You shall not bear false witness against your neighbor.
9. You shall not covet your neighbor's wife.
10. You shall not covet anything that belongs to your neighbor.

THE TWO GREAT COMMANDMENTS

You shall love the Lord your God
  with all your heart,
  with all your soul,
  with all your mind
  and with all your strength.
You shall love your neighbor as yourself.

THE SEVEN SACRAMENTS

Baptism
Confirmation
Holy Eucharist
Penance
Anointing of the Sick
Holy Orders
Matrimony

SPECIAL DUTIES OF CATHOLIC CHRISTIANS

1. To keep holy the day of the Lord's Resurrection: to worship God by participating in Mass every Sunday and holyday of obligation*: to avoid those activities that would hinder renewal of soul and body, e.g., needless work and business activities, unnecessary shopping, etc.
2. To lead a sacramental life: to receive Holy Communion frequently and the Sacrament of Penance regularly
   —minimally, to receive the Sacrament of Penance at least once a year (annual confession is obligatory only if serious sin is involved).
   —minimally, to receive Holy Communion at least once a year, between the First Sunday of Lent and Trinity Sunday.
3. To study Catholic teaching in preparation for the Sacrament of Confirmation, to be confirmed, and then to continue to study and advance the cause of Christ.
4. To observe the marriage laws of the Church: to give religious training (by example and word) to one's children; to use parish schools and religious education programs.
5. To strengthen and support the Church: one's own parish community and parish priests; the worldwide Church and the Holy Father.
6. To do penance, including abstaining from meat and fasting from food on the appointed days.
7. To join in the missionary spirit and apostolate of the Church.

*In the United States, these days are: Christmas, January 1, Ascension Thursday, the Assumption (Aug. 15), All Saints' Day (Nov. 1), the Immaculate Conception (Dec. 8).

THE EIGHT BEATITUDES

1. Blest are the poor in spirit: the reign of God is theirs.
2. Blest are the sorrowing: they shall be consoled.
3. Blest are the lowly: they shall inherit the land.
4. Blest are they who hunger and thirst for holiness: they shall have their fill.
5. Blest are they who show mercy: mercy shall be theirs.
6. Blest are the single-hearted: for they shall see God.
7. Blest are the peacemakers: they shall be called sons of God.
8. Blest are those persecuted for holiness' sake: the reign of God is theirs.

THE WORKS OF MERCY

Spiritual

1. To admonish the sinner
2. To instruct the ignorant
3. To counsel the doubtful
4. To comfort the sorrowful
5. To bear wrongs patiently
6. To forgive all injuries
7. To pray for the living and the dead

Corporal

1. To feed the hungry
2. To give drink to the thirsty
3. To clothe the naked
4. To visit the imprisoned
5. To shelter the homeless
6. To visit the sick
7. To bury the dead

Some Basic Truths of Our Faith

GOD AND OURSELVES

1. Who is God?
God is the Creator of heaven and earth, of all that is seen and unseen.

2. What does "Creator" mean?
A Creator is one who makes from nothing. The only Creator is God.

3. What is God like?
God is a pure spirit. He is completely perfect—all-knowing, all-good, all-powerful and all-loving.

4. What is the mystery of the Blessed Trinity?
The mystery of the Blessed Trinity is one God in three divine persons: the Father, the Son and the Holy Spirit.

5. Does God care about us?
God cares about us very much. He keeps us in existence, helps us in everything we do, and watches over us with love.

6. How do we know about God?
We know about God through what He has created and especially through the Catholic Church and the Bible.

7. What is the Bible?
The Bible is the Holy Book in which God speaks to us through the words of men who wrote what He wanted them to write.

8. What is the meaning of life?
God gave us life so that we will use it to know Him, love Him and serve Him now and be happy with Him forever in heaven.

9. How do we learn to know, love and serve God?
We learn to know, love and serve God from the teachings and examples of Jesus Christ.

10. Who is Jesus Christ?
Jesus Christ is God the Son, who became man for us while remaining God.

11. Where do we find the teachings and examples of Jesus Christ?
We find the teachings and examples of Jesus Christ in the Bible, especially in the four Gospels.

12. What is the Incarnation?
The Incarnation is the taking of a human nature by God the Son.

13. Why did God become man?
God became man to save us from our sins, give us His grace, and teach us what we must believe and do to reach heaven.

14. What is the Redemption?
The Redemption is Jesus' death and resurrection, by which He made up for our sins and won for us the help we need for reaching heaven.

15. What do we learn from Jesus' choice of death for our sake?
From Jesus' choice of death for our sake we learn how much He loves us and how terrible sin is.

SIN

16. What is sin?
Sin is disobedience to God and His laws.

17. What is original sin?
Original sin is the lack of grace with which each of us came into the world because of the sin of our first parents.

18. What is personal sin?
Personal sin is personal disobedience to God's law through a willful thought, desire, word, action or omission.

19. What does sin do to a person?
Serious (mortal) sin drives out God's grace. Lesser (venial) sin weakens the person's friendship with God.

GRACE

20. What is grace?
Grace is a gift that God gives us to bring us closer to Him.

21. What is sanctifying grace?
Sanctifying grace is a sharing in God's own life that makes us holy (close to Him).

22. What is actual grace?
Actual grace is light for our mind and strength for our will, which God gives us whenever we need it.

23. Why is grace important?
Grace is important because we need God's life and help in order to please Him in life and enter His happiness after death.

THE VIRGIN MARY

24. Who is Mary?
Mary is the Mother of Jesus and therefore the Mother of God.

25. Why do we call Mary our Mother?
We call Mary our Mother because Jesus Himself made her the spiritual Mother of the Church and of each one of us.

26. What is the Immaculate Conception?
The Immaculate Conception is Mary's freedom from original sin from the first moment of her existence.

27. What is the Assumption?
The Assumption is the taking up of the Blessed Virgin Mary into heaven body and soul by God's power.

THE CATHOLIC CHURCH

28. What is the Catholic Church?
The Catholic Church is God's people, whom He has joined together in the same beliefs, laws and sacraments under the Pope.

29. Why did Jesus Christ found the Church?
Jesus Christ founded the Church in order to continue His mission on earth—that is, to save mankind.

30. Who was St. Peter?
St. Peter was the apostle whom Jesus chose to be the first Pope.

31. Who is the Pope?
The Pope is Jesus' representative (vicar) on earth.

32. Is the Pope the head of the Church?
The Pope is the *visible* head of the Church and Jesus is its *invisible* Head.

33. Why did Jesus give us the Pope?
Jesus gave us the Pope for the sake of the unity of the Church.

34. Who are the bishops?
The bishops are the leaders of the Church, united with the Pope and under him.

35. What does Jesus do for us through the Church?
Through the Church Jesus gives us grace and teaches us what we must believe and do in order to reach heaven.

36. What is infallibility?
Infallibility is God-given freedom from making mistakes in matters of faith and morals, which belongs under certain conditions to the Pope and the bishops united with him.

37. Why is infallibility important?
Infallibility is important because it guarantees to the Catholic Church the sureness of God's truth.

38. Why is it important to live a real Catholic life?
It is important to live a real Catholic life because the Catholic Church has the sureness of Christ's truth and the fullness of His grace.

THE SACRAMENTS

39. How does the life of grace come to us?
The life of grace comes to us chiefly through the Mass and the other sacraments.

40. What is the Mass?
The Mass is the sacrifice of the cross taking place today; a memorial of Jesus' death and resurrection; a holy meal in which we receive Christ Himself.

41. What are the sacraments?
The sacraments are seven special actions of Jesus through which He gives us His Spirit to make us holy by grace.

42. What are the names of the seven sacraments?
The seven sacraments are: Baptism, Confirmation, Holy Eucharist, Penance, Anointing of the Sick, Holy Orders and Matrimony.

43. What is Baptism?
Baptism is the sacrament in which Jesus sends us His Spirit to free us from sin, seal us as Christians, and give us His grace.

44. What did the grace of Baptism do for us?

The grace of Baptism made us God's children, heirs of heaven, living members of the Church and temples of the Blessed Trinity, the Father, the Son and the Holy Spirit.

45. What is Confirmation?

Confirmation is the sacrament in which the Holy Spirit joins us more closely to Jesus and His Church, strengthens our faith, and seals us as Christ's witnesses.

46. What is the Eucharist?

The Eucharist is the sacrament of Jesus' real and complete presence, in which He renews His sacrifice, comes to us as Holy Communion, and remains close to us in our churches.

47. What is Penance?

Penance is the sacrament in which Jesus forgives our sins, strengthens or renews our friendship with Himself and His people, and gives us the strength to do better.

48. How do we receive the sacrament of Penance?

To receive the sacrament of Penance we: remember our sins; are sorry for them; intend not to commit them again; tell them in confession; say or do our penance.

49. What are mortal and venial sins?

Mortal sins are serious disobediences to God and His law, which must be told in confession. Venial sins are less serious disobediences.

50. When is a sin mortal?

A sin is mortal when the person knew before or while committing it that it was seriously wrong, yet freely and deliberately decided to do it.

51. What is the Anointing of the Sick?

The Anointing of the Sick is the sacrament in which Jesus brings healing of soul and often of body to sick or injured people in danger of death or to the elderly.

52. What is Holy Orders?

Holy Orders is the sacrament through which Jesus gives His Spirit to men to seal them as deacons, priests and bishops and to give them the powers that belong to each position.

53. What is Matrimony?

Matrimony is the sacrament through which Jesus blesses a marriage and gives the couple the grace to love one another faithfully throughout life, to love their children and to raise their children as good Christians.

54. Why are the sacraments important?

The sacraments are important because they are the chief ways in which we receive or grow in God's grace and are strengthened to live as we should.

THE COMMANDMENTS OF GOD

55. What are God's ten commandments?

God's ten commandments are laws which guide us in living the way all human beings should live.

56. What does God tell us in the first commandment?

In the first commandment God tells us that we should pray to Him, believe His teachings, trust Him and love Him.

57. What are some of the sins forbidden by the first commandment?

Some of the sins forbidden by the first commandment are: giving up the Catholic religion; refusing to believe one or more of the Church's teachings; reading books or pamphlets against the Catholic faith; practicing superstition.

58. What does God tell us in the second commandment?

In the second commandment God tells us to speak with respect of Him, of holy things, of holy places and of persons close to Him.

59. What are some of the sins forbidden by the second commandment?

Some of the sins forbidden by the second commandment are: using the names of God or Jesus in a wrong way; insulting God or religion; perjury (lying when under oath).

60. What does God tell us in the third commandment?

In the third commandment God tells us to make Sunday special by worshiping Him at Mass (which may also be done on Saturday evening) and by taking the rest we need.

61. What are some of the sins forbidden by the third commandment?

Some of the sins forbidden by the third commandment are: missing Mass on Sunday (Saturday evening); being late for Mass on purpose; doing unnecessary hard work on Sunday.

62. What does God tell us in the fourth commandment?

In the fourth commandment God tells us to love, respect, obey and help our parents and to respect and obey others who are in charge of us, such as teachers, the leaders of our Church and country, etc.

63. What are some of the sins forbidden by the fourth commandment?

Some of the sins forbidden by the fourth commandment are: disobeying one's parents; hating, striking or insulting them; speaking or acting unkindly toward them; causing them anger or sorrow.

64. What does God tell us in the fifth commandment?

In the fifth commandment God tells us to look after the life, health, safety and spiritual good of ourselves and others.

65. What are some of the sins forbidden by the fifth commandment?

Some of the sins forbidden by the fifth commandment are: murder; abortion; suicide; euthanasia (mercy killing); drunkenness; drug taking; unnecessary risk of life; anger; hatred; fighting; leading others to sin.

66. What does God tell us in the sixth and ninth commandments?

In the sixth and ninth commandments God tells us to respect His gift of sex by avoiding the thoughts, desires and actions that are permitted only to married people, and by avoiding conversations, ways of dressing, pictures, books, etc., which could lead us or others to sin.

67. What are some of the sins forbidden by the sixth and ninth commandments?

Some of the sins forbidden by the sixth and ninth commandments are: adultery[1], fornication[2], contraception[3], homosexuality, masturbation, deliberate thoughts, words or actions that arouse sexual feelings.

68. How can we help ourselves to keep the sixth and ninth commandments?

We can help ourselves to keep the sixth and ninth commandments by praying often, especially to the Virgin Mary; by receiving Penance and the Eucharist often; by keeping ourselves busy; and by avoiding persons, places or things that might tempt us to sin.

69. What does God tell us in the seventh and tenth commandments?

In the seventh and tenth commandments God tells us to take care of our own things, to respect what belongs to others and to make up for any stealing or harming of property that we have done deliberately.

70. What are some of the sins forbidden by the seventh and tenth commandments?

Some of the sins forbidden by the seventh and tenth commandments are: stealing; wanting to steal; unjustly keeping what is not ours; cheating; willfully damaging the property of others; wasting time or materials when working; not paying what we owe.

71. What does God tell us in the eighth commandment?

In the eighth commandment God tells us to say only what is true and good, and if we have injured someone's reputation to make up for the harm we have done.

72. What are some of the sins forbidden by the eighth commandment?

Some of the sins forbidden by the eighth commandment are: lying; insulting; harming someone's reputation; criticizing unfairly; not keeping secrets that we should keep.

---

1. Sexual relations between two persons, one of whom is married to someone else.

2. Sexual relations between unmarried persons.

3. Artificial birth control.

LISTING of BIBLICAL PICTURES

(illustrations by G. DeLuca)
13 – The birth of Isaac
14 – Abraham and Isaac on the way to offer sacrifice
 – Abraham about to sacrifice Isaac
15 – Abraham worshiping God
16 – Joseph in prison
17 – Joseph's brothers come to ask for grain
 – Joseph reveals who he is
18 – Moses and the burning bush
19 – Moses' staff changes into a snake
 – Locusts and sicknesses plague the Egyptians
21 – The Israelites leave Egypt
22 – The waters catch the Egyptians
23 – Moses striking the rock for water
24 – Moses with the commandments
 – The Israelite camp
26 – Moses re-climbing Sinai
27 – Aaron becomes an Israelite priest
29 – An Israelite priest offering sacrifice
 – The ark of the covenant
32 – Battling for Canaan
33 – Joshua's prayer
 – Samson fighting the Philistines with a donkey's jawbone
34 – Gideon's "attack" on the Midianite camp
 – Gideon's soldiers cheer him
35 – Ruth gathering grain in the field of Boaz
 – Obed – Naomi's pride and joy
36 – Samuel's mother brings him to Eli
 – Samuel preaching
 – Samuel presents Saul to the people
37 – David and Goliath
 – The crowds hail David as a hero
38 – Saul attempts to kill David
 – David cuts a piece off the king's garment to show how close he came to him
 – David has the ark brought to Jerusalem
40 – The anointing of Solomon as king
41 – Jeroboam's anger at the prophet
42 – The fall of the northern kingdom
43 – Jeremiah lowered into a cistern
44 – The burning of Jerusalem
 – The captives on the way to Babylon
46 – The reading of Cyrus' decree
 – The return of the exiles
 – The rebuilding of Jerusalem's walls in the face of opposition
48 – The desecration of the temple
 – The dying Mattathias and his sons
49 – Judas Maccabeus and his men weeping over the temple
53 – Moses bringing a plague on Egypt by God's power
 – David worshiping the Lord
 – The prophets Ezekiel and Isaiah
54 – A prophet foretelling the New Covenant
55 – Mary visits Elizabeth
58 – The Holy Family flees into Egypt
 – A scene from Jesus' boyhood at Nazareth
59 – At twelve, Jesus goes to Jerusalem with Mary and Joseph
 – Jesus among the religious teachers
60 – John the Baptizer points out Jesus
 – Jesus and His two first followers
61 – Jesus healing a leper
62 – The sermon on the mount
65 – Jesus sleeping – awakened by apostles
 – The multiplication of the loaves
 – The sick beg Jesus for help
66 – Jesus preaching about the Eucharist
67 – Jesus preaching from a boat
 – The apostle John
70 – Mary praising God's goodness
 – Jesus and Mary working at Nazareth
71 – Jesus and the twelve apostles
72 – Jesus and Peter in the fishing boat
73 – Jesus' promise to Peter, "the Rock"
74 – "Lord, this mustn't happen to You!"
75 – Jesus praying and preaching
 – The good Samaritan parable
78 – Martha and Mary
79 – Jesus teaching prayer
 – Jesus going off alone to pray
80 – The turmoil over Jesus
 – Jesus preaching in Jerusalem
 – Jesus replying to His enemies
82 – Jesus healing the man born blind
83 – The Good Shepherd
85 – Angry Pharisees
 – An attempt to stone Jesus
86 – Jesus comforts Martha and Mary
87 – The raising of Lazarus
88 – The conspiracy to put Jesus to death
89 – Jesus enters Jerusalem in triumph
92 – Judas leaves the supper room
93 – Jesus institutes the Eucharist
102 – Jesus brought to Pilate
103 – The mob cries for His death
104 – "Look at the man!"
 – Jesus is nailed to the cross
105 – Jesus' death on the cross
 – His body is taken down
107 – Peter and John at the tomb
 – The resurrection
 – Jesus and Mary Magdalene
108 – Jesus appears to the apostles in Jerusalem
109 – He talks with His apostles in Galilee
112 – Mary and the apostles at prayer
113 – Peter preaching about Jesus
 – Peter and the lame beggar
114 – The religious leaders discuss the apostles
 – Stephen's martyrdom
 – Saul's approval of Stephen's death
115 – Saul as persecutor
118 – Saul's instruction by Jesus
 – His escape from Damascus
 – Saul's meeting with Peter
120 – Peter in the home of Cornelius
121 – Paul and Barnabas sail for Cyprus
122 – The Lystrans try to worship the missionaries
123 – The Council of Jerusalem
 – Paul and Silas in prison
125 – Paul preaching to the Gentiles
 – Writing an epistle (letter)
126 – Scenes of difficulties Paul had come up against
129 – The fierce storm during Paul's voyage to Rome
 – Paul shakes the poisonous snake off his hand
130 – Paul writing from prison
131 – The crucifixion of Peter
132 – John writing

Glossary

A

actual graces—temporary helps from the Holy Spirit which make us able to know and do what God expects of us at a certain moment

adore—praise and worship God

adultery—the sin of sexual intercourse between a married person and someone who is not his or her marriage partner

Advocate—a name given to the Holy Spirit, meaning "one who pleads for our needs"

alleluia — a Hebrew word — now used in Christian worship — which means "praise God" or "may God be praised"

altar—a table or similar structure on which sacrifice is offered

Ammonites—a tribe of Arameans who established themselves east of the Jordan about the same time that the Israelites took over Canaan

angels—spirits without bodies, created by God

anoint—to sign with blessed oil, which shows that power, strength or healing is being given by God

Anointing of the Sick—the sacrament through which Jesus gives comfort to sick or injured people in danger of death and to the elderly, by giving grace and strength of soul, healing spiritual weaknesses and lessening punishment for sins (if it is God's will, bodily health is also restored)

apocalyptic—a type of symbolic writing having to do with a great struggle between good and evil

apostles—certain of Jesus' disciples whom He chose to be the leaders of His Church

apparition—a sudden, unexpected appearance

Aramaic—the language of the Arameans, which was closely related to Hebrew; by Jesus' time it had become the ordinary language of the Galileans, the Samaritans and the Jewish people living east of the River Jordan

Arameans—a large group of peoples (from whom the Hebrews may have originated) who founded several small states in the region of Syria and northwestern Mesopotamia

ark—the name given to Noah's boat; sometimes the Church is compared to the ark

ark of the covenant—a wooden chest, overlaid with gold, which contained the stone tablets of the commandments and symbolized both the covenant and God's presence among His people; the ark was Yahweh's throne

Ascension — Jesus' visible departure from this earth; the Thursday on which we remember this event (a holyday of obligation, 40 days after Easter)

Assyrians—a warlike people who took over northern and central Mesopotamia around the 17th century B.C. They gradually built up an empire, which was crushed at the end of the 7th century B.C. by the Babylonians

atone—to make up for sin

B

baptism—a religious ceremony involving dipping in water or the pouring or sprinkling of water

Baptism—the sacrament in which Jesus sends us His Spirit, who frees us from sin and gives us the grace by which we become God's children, heirs of heaven, members of the Church and temples of the Blessed Trinity

baptism of blood—the reception of grace by an unbaptized person because he or she gives his life for love of Christ or a Christian virtue

baptism of desire—the reception of grace because of perfect love of God and the desire to do His will; in other words, if the person knew of Baptism and was able to receive it, he would be baptized

beatitudes—promises of happiness as a reward for following Jesus in a more perfect way

Bible—the holy Book—or library of books—in which God speaks to us through the writings of men who wrote what He wanted them to write

bishops—leaders of the Church, who hold the place of the apostles

Blessed Trinity—one God in three divine Persons

Blessed Virgin—one of the names given to Mary, the Mother of Jesus

blessings—words and actions by which a thing or person is placed under the care of God

Body of Christ—the Eucharist

body of Christ—Christ's followers, joined together by the Holy Spirit and grace

C

Caesar—the name of a famous Roman general, which later became a title of the Roman emperor

Canaan—one of the earlier names for the land of Palestine—Jesus' homeland

Canaanites—early inhabitants of the land promised by God to Abraham and his descendants

Cenacle—a name given to the room where the Last Supper was held

Chaldeans—Babylonians who threw off the yoke of Assyria and created an empire; these were the conquerors of Judah, who took many of the chosen people into exile

charity—a power by which we love God above everything and we love all other people for His sake

cherubim—two golden statues which spread their wings over the ark of the covenant, indicating the ark's importance

chosen people—the Hebrews (Israelites, Jewish people), whom God especially chose to prepare the world for the coming of the Savior

Christ—"the Anointed One"—a Greek translation of the Hebrew word "Messiah"

Christian—a baptized follower of Jesus Christ

Christmas—the holyday of obligation on which we celebrate Jesus' birth

Church—a word meaning gathering or community, used as the name of all Jesus' baptized followers united in the same faith, sacrifice and sacraments under the Pope and the bishops united with him (the Church on earth may be called the pilgrim Church; the souls in purgatory, the suffering Church; the Church in heaven, the blessed Church or Church of the blessed)

Communion—the receiving of Jesus in the Holy Eucharist

communion of saints—the communication of spiritual help among God's faithful people on earth, in purgatory and in heaven

Confirmation—the sacrament in which the Holy Spirit comes to us in a special way to join us more closely to Jesus and His Church and seal and strengthen us as Christ's witnesses

Consecration—the sacred part of the Mass in which Jesus Christ through the ministry and power of ordained priests changes bread and wine into His own Body and Blood

convert—a person who has changed from one religion to another

council (ecumenical)—a special meeting of bishops from all over the world, united with the Pope; by the power of the Holy Spirit, ecumenical councils teach infallibly

covenant—a lasting alliance or agreement of friendship

covet—to want to take

creation—the bringing of something out of nothing—which only God can do

crucifixion—death on a cross

D

Davidic—an adjective referring to David and his descendants

deacon—a man ordained to help priests by baptizing, distributing Communion, preaching God's Word, etc.

death—the separation of soul and body, when the body becomes lifeless while the soul continues to live

decalogue—another name for the ten commandments

devil—any of the angels who turned against God and now tempt human beings to turn against Him

diaspora—the Jewish people scattered among the Gentile nations

diocese—a territory made up of parishes placed by the Pope under the care of a Church leader called an "ordinary" (usually a bishop)

disciples—pupils or followers

divine—referring to God

divine providence—God's loving, fatherly care for His creatures

Divine Tradition—see Tradition

dynasty—a series of rulers who belong to the same family

E

Easter—the Church's greatest day of celebration—on which we rejoice over Jesus' resurrection

Easter Vigil—a celebration held on Holy Saturday night in preparation for the feast of Easter. Its high point is the Mass of the Lord's resurrection

Edomites—peoples who settled south of the Dead Sea around 1300 B.C.; at times they were enemies of the Israelites

Egyptians—through the centuries, powerful neighbors of the Israelites, with whom they generally were on good terms

epistle—a letter which has become a book of the New Testament

Essenes—members of a strict sect (division) of the Jewish religion; many of them lived at Qumran, near the Dead Sea

eternity—the condition in which there is no beginning and no end

Eucharist—the sacrament of Jesus' complete presence, in which (under the appearances of bread and wine) He offers His sacrifice again, comes to His people as their spiritual food, and remains in our midst to be close to us and help us

evangelist—one of the Gospel writers

evangelize—to spread the Good News (the Gospel message)

Exile—the period of the chosen people's captivity in Babylon

exile—a person who has to live away from his or her own homeland

Exodus—the journey of the Israelites from slavery in Egypt to the Promised Land (Canaan); the book of the Old Testament that tells about the Exodus and the events that led up to it

F

faith—a God-given power and habit by which we believe in Him and everything He has taught us

Faith—what we believe; our Catholic religion

Father—the first Person of the Trinity, who watches over us with the love of a father

fortitude—the cardinal virtue by which a person does what is good and right in spite of any difficulty

G

Galilee—the name used in Jesus' time for the northern region of Palestine, which lay west of the sea of Galilee

Gentiles—people who were (are) neither Jewish by ancestry nor followers of the Jewish religion

Gospels—the "Good News" of Jesus and of our salvation by Him as told by Matthew, Mark, Luke and John

grace (sanctifying)—the grace (gift of God) that is a sharing in His own life and makes us holy—distinguished from such other graces as actual grace (temporary help for our mind and/or will)

Greek (language)—The language that was spread throughout much of the Near East after Alexander the Great's conquest; later, it was used widely throughout the Roman Empire. Greek was the original language of most of the New Testament and some parts of the Old Testament

H

Hanukkah—the Jewish "feast of lights," held yearly in remembrance of the rededication of the temple by Judas Maccabeus

heaven—everlasting life and happiness with God

Hebrew (language)—the language spoken by the Hebrews or Israelites for many years, until in some regions it was replaced by a related language, Aramaic. Much of the Old Testament was written in Hebrew

Hebrews—the people descended from Abraham, whom God chose to prepare the world for the coming of the Savior (also called **Israelites** around the time of the Exodus and **Jewish people** after the Exile)

hell—everlasting suffering and separation from God

Hermes—a Greek god, corresponding to the Roman Mercury (the Lystrans mistook St. Paul for Hermes)

high priest—the leader of all the Israelite (Jewish) priests—the only one permitted to enter the Holy of Holies in the temple

Holy Bible—the Sacred Scriptures—God's written Word

Holy City—the name given to Jerusalem, which is holy to Jews because of its past association with the temple and the ark, to Christians because of Jesus' death and resurrection, and also to Moslems

Holy Land—Palestine, the homeland of Jesus

Holy Orders—the sacrament through which Jesus gives His Spirit to men to make them deacons, priests and bishops and to give them the powers that belong to each status

Holy Spirit—the third Person of the Trinity, sent by the Father and the Son to live in us and in the Church; the Spirit of truth and love

hope—the power and habit of trusting that our all-powerful and faithful God will bring us to eternal happiness if we do our part

hosanna—a shout of joy taken from the Psalms which means, "Do save us!"

humility—the virtue by which we truly know ourselves and see that whatever is good in us comes from God

Hyksos—peoples from Canaan or southern Syria who took control of Egypt around the 18th century B.C. but were eventually expelled. The Hyksos were in power when Jacob's family moved to Egypt

I

Immaculate Conception—freedom from original sin from the very first moment of existence—a privilege that God gave to the Blessed Mother; the holyday of obligation (December 8) on which this event is honored

Incarnation—the taking of a human body and soul (human nature) by God the Son

infallibility—freedom from making a mistake when teaching a truth of faith or right living (a gift given by the Holy Spirit to the Pope and the bishops united with him)

inspiration—the special guidance that the Holy Spirit gave to the Bible's human authors, so that they wrote everything God wanted them to write and only that

Israel—the name God gave to Jacob; the name of the Hebrew nation before its division into two kingdoms; the name of the northern kingdom after the division

Israelites—the name by which Abraham's descendants, the Jewish people, were called around the time of the Exodus and during their first centuries in Palestine

J

Jerusalem—the city that King David captured from the Jebusites and made his capital. After the division of the chosen people into two kingdoms, Jerusalem remained the capital of Judah. (See also Holy City.)

Jesus—a Greek form of the Hebrew name Joshua, meaning "God saves"—the personal name of our Savior

Jews—the name by which the chosen people were known after the Exile (derived from the tribe of Judah, to which most of the returned exiles belonged).
Also used for followers of the Jewish religion; a Gentile could join this religion by fulfilling a number of required conditions

Judah—the name of the tribe of Israel to which David belonged and from which Christ was descended; also the name of the southern kingdom after the division

Judaism—the highly-organized religion of the Jewish people after the Exile. Judaism centered about the temple, the priesthood and the Scriptures

Judea—a region of Palestine during Jesus' time; it corresponded roughly to the old kingdom of Judah. Jerusalem was located in Judea

judges—charismatic (God-gifted) military leaders whom Yahweh inspired to lead His people in battle during their difficult early years in Canaan

judgment—the moment at which Jesus Christ will tell each of us what reward or punishment we will receive for the good or evil we have done

just—fair

justice—fairness; giving everyone what he or she deserves

K

kingdom of God—both the kingdom of God in this world (the Church) and that of the next world (heaven)

L

Lake Genesareth—another name for the Sea of Galilee

Last Supper—the meal celebrated by Jesus and His apostles at which He gave us the Eucharist

Latin—the language of ancient Rome and its people, which became the official language of the Church

lay person—in the usual sense, a member of the Church who is not a priest or religious

leaven—yeast, which spreads through dough and gradually changes it; hence, anything that gradually changes something else from within, as the Gospel should do to society

Levi—the tribe of Israel to which the priests and their helpers belonged

Levites—helpers of the Jewish priests

Liturgy of the Eucharist—the part of the Mass in which we offer our gifts to God, Jesus becomes present and we receive Him in Communion

Liturgy of the Word—the part of the Mass that includes the Scripture readings and our responses to them

love—charity—a power by which we love God above everything and all other people for His sake

M

Maccabees—a name given to the family and supporters of Judas "Maccabeus" and even to other heroes of the period in which Judas lived. The name probably means "hammer"

martyrs—persons who allow themselves to be put to death because of their beliefs

Mass—the very sacrifice of the cross taking place today on our altars; a memorial of Jesus' death, resurrection and ascension; a holy covenant meal in which we receive Jesus Himself

Master — a title meaning "teacher" by which the apostles called Jesus

Matrimony — the sacrament through which Jesus blesses a marriage, giving the couple the right to call upon Him for help in loving and being loyal to one another for life and in raising the children God will send them

mediator — a "go-between"; someone who relays instructions, asks favors for another, etc.

merciful — having or showing kindness or forgiveness

Messiah — "the Anointed One" — a king descended from David who was to establish (and did establish) God's lasting kingdom in the world

messianic age — the time of the coming of the Messiah

Midianites — a nomadic people who at various times were to be found in the deserts south and east of Canaan and sometimes in Canaan itself — among the first peoples ever to use camels in warfare

miracle — an event that takes place outside of the ordinary working of nature's laws — something only God could do, because He made the laws

mission — a purpose, which for Christ and the Christian is the saving of the world; a Christian community established to give non-Christian peoples a chance to learn about Jesus and salvation

missionary — a person who is sent to share the truths of religion with others

Moabites — a people who lived on the fertile plain east of the Dead Sea

moral — having to do with right and wrong, with conduct pleasing to God

morals — standards regarding what is right and wrong

mystery — a great truth made known by God which our limited minds will never be able to fully understand

mystical body — the real but unseen union of members of the Church (living and dead) with Jesus and one another, through the grace-giving activity of the Holy Spirit

N

Nazarene (Nazorean) — a name by which Jesus was known; it comes from the name of the village in which He spent most of His "hidden life"

new covenant — the lasting covenant between God and men that was made by Jesus Christ

New Testament — the second part of the Bible, which tells about the life and teachings of Jesus and the life of the early Church

O

obedience — the virtue by which a person obeys someone (a parent, a teacher, a religious superior...) who represents God for that person

Old Testament — the first part of the Bible, which tells about the preparation of the chosen people for the coming of the Savior, Jesus Christ

original sin — the lack of grace with which each of us comes into the world, because our first parents lost grace both for themselves and for us

P

pagan — pertaining to people who do not believe in the one, true God

pagans — people who have no religion or believe in more than one God

parable — a story that teaches a truth of religion or a principle of right living

Paraclete — a name given to the Holy Spirit — meaning "one who pleads for our needs" (see Romans 8:26-27)

paschal — referring to either the Jewish Passover or the Christian Easter

paschal lamb — the lamb (or kid goat) that the Israelites would sacrifice to God at Passover time

paschal mystery — Jesus' death and resurrection; the Last Supper, passion, death, resurrection, ascension and sending of the Holy Spirit

passion — the sufferings of Jesus before His death

Passover — the Jewish feast held yearly in memory of the Israelites' liberation from slavery in Egypt

patience — the virtue of calmly enduring suffering or hardship

patriarchs — fathers of a family or tribe; the first fathers of the Hebrew people: Abraham, Isaac and Jacob

Penance — the sacrament of God's loving forgiveness, by which we are set free from sin and at least eternal punishment, grow in God's grace and are strengthened to avoid sin and lead holier lives

Pentecost — the Sunday, seven weeks after Easter, on which we celebrate the memory of the Holy Spirit's descent upon the apostles

Perea — at the time of Jesus, one of the Roman divisions of Palestine east of the Jordan

persecution — suffering caused by others because they are against what a person stands for

Persians — a people who settled in what today would be called northeastern Iran and in the 6th century B.C. conquered much of the Near East

pharaoh — the title of each ruler of ancient Egypt

Pharisees — the main religious leaders of the Jewish people at the time of Jesus

Philistines — a people from the lands around the Aegean Sea who settled in southwestern Canaan around the year 1200 B.C., about the same time the Israelite conquest was beginning. They became a great threat to the Israelites because they knew how to make iron weapons

philosophers — people who study the basic "whys" of the universe and of man himself

Phoenicia — the land of Byblos, Tyre and Sidon, stretching northward from Mt. Carmel along the Mediterranean coast

pilgrim — traveler on a holy journey

pilgrimage — journey to a holy place for a holy purpose

plague — an epidemic or any similar disaster that affects a great number of people

Pope — the chief teacher and leader of the Catholic Church; Peter's successor; the one who holds the place of Jesus in the Church

prayer — talking with God with mind and heart and often with voice as well

presbyters — members of the early Church who ranked above deacons but below bishops. They seem to have had much the same functions as today's priests

priest — one who represents the people in their worship of God; priests offer sacrifice

prophecy — the relating (telling) of messages from God as to what He asks of His people; also, the definite foretelling of a future event that no human being could predict without God's help

prophet — a person who spoke for God or interpreted His message

providence — the loving care of God for His creatures, especially human beings; His way of "making things work together for good" (cf. Romans 8:28)

prudence — the cardinal virtue by which a person puts heaven before everything else, thinks carefully before acting, makes wise choices and does things well

psalms — religious poems that may be prayed or sung

Ptolemies — the successors of Ptolemy, one of the generals of Alexander the Great. They ruled Egypt from the late 4th century B.C. until its conquest by Rome

public life (of Jesus) — the time during which Jesus went about preaching the Good News, healing, and instructing His apostles

purgatory — a condition of suffering after death in which souls make up for their sins before they enter heaven

Q

Qumran — a settlement on the northwest shore of the Dead Sea, which existed from about 135 B.C. to 68 A.D. It was built by the Essenes, and in nearby caves many ancient writings (the "Dead Sea scrolls") have been found; these tell us much about the Essenes themselves and the times in which they lived

R

rabbi — at the time of Jesus, the title for any outstanding teacher of religion; now the title of a Jewish clergyman or spiritual leader

redeem — to set free (from sin)

Redemption — "buying back" — the rescue or ransom of all of us by Jesus, who laid down His life to set us free from sin

reign of God — the kingdom of God on earth and in heaven — the Church and everyone who belongs to it completely or partially

religion — belief in God, obedience to Him and worship of Him; the virtue by which we give God reverence, obedience and worship

reparation — making up for one's own sins or those of others

repentance — sorrow for sins and the intention of not sinning again

resurrection — Jesus' rising from the dead by His own power; the raising of all bodies from the dead at the end of the world, rejoined with their souls by God

revelation — the truths of religion which God has made known to us through Scripture and Tradition

rite — the way in which worship is carried out — that is, the words and actions used

S

Sabbath — the Israelite (Jewish) day to give special worship to God and to rest from work

sacraments — the actions of Jesus — the chief ways in which He gives us His Spirit to make us holy — visible signs of His invisible grace

Sacred Tradition — see Tradition

sacrifice — giving oneself to God through the sign of offering Him something precious

Sadducees — a sect (division) of the Jewish religion at the time of Jesus which was less strict than the Pharisees; many wealthy and priestly families belonged to this sect

saint — a holy person on earth or in heaven, especially someone who grew so close to God on earth that the Church declared him or her a saint after death

salvation — the condition of being saved (set free from sin and brought to God)

salvation history — God's loving activity throughout human history to free people from sin and help them to lead good lives so that they will be happy in this life and in the next

Samaria — in Old Testament times, the most famous capital city of the northern kingdom; in Jesus' time, the name of the region of Palestine north of Judea and south of Galilee

Samaritans — a mixed race descended from a few Israelites who had inter-married with other peoples brought in after the Assyrian conquest. Not following all the Jewish teachings, the Samaritans were looked down upon by the Jews — nor were the Jews liked by the Samaritans

satan — another name for the devil — a fallen angel

save — to set free from sin; to bring to God and heaven

savior — one who sets free

Savior — Jesus Christ, who died to save everyone who would accept His salvation

Scribes — experts regarding the Jewish law

Scripture (or **Scriptures**) — the written Word of God, the Bible

Sea of Reeds — the body of water through which the Israelites passed when fleeing from Pharaoh's army. It was probably somewhere near the present-day Suez Canal

Sea of Tiberias — another name for the Sea of Galilee

Seleucids — the successors of Seleucus, a general of Alexander the Great. Ruling from Antioch, in 198 the Seleucids gained control of Palestine, which they held until the Maccabean revolt

seminomads — tent dwellers who lived on the fringes of settled areas, moving whenever it was necessary to find new pasture lands for their flocks and herds

sepulcher — a burial place — a tomb

sermon — a talk given for religious instruction

Sermon on the Mount — Jesus' preaching of many of the teachings of the new covenant, as recorded in St. Matthew's Gospel (chapters 5-7)

sign — something that can be heard and/or seen, etc., and which stands for something else (hence, the sacraments are signs); also, the name St. John gives to Jesus' miracles—signs of God's activity and power

sin—disobedience to God and His laws. (**Mortal** sin is a serious offense, which drives God's grace out of a soul; **venial** sin is a less serious offense, which weakens a person's friendship with God.)

Son—the second Person of the Trinity, who became man, died and rose to save us; He is the God-man, Jesus Christ

soul—the spirit which together with a body makes up a human being

spirit—something living but not material

Sumerians—a people of Mesopotamia who developed a very high civilization well before 2000 B.C.; Abraham may have come from Sumer (in the 19th century B.C.)

supernatural—what is above the powers of nature

T

tabernacle—in the Old Testament, the tent that sheltered the ark of the covenant; now, the box-like enclosure in which the Blessed Sacrament is kept

temperance—the cardinal virtue by which a person exercises self-control with regard to food, sex, etc.

temple—the center of Jewish worship from the time of Solomon until 587 B.C. and again from around 515 B.C. until its destruction by the Romans in 70 A.D. (except for the brief period of desecration at the time of the Maccabees)

temptation—something that makes sin attractive

theophany—an appearance of God to human beings in some way, as in the burning bush or at Jesus' baptism

tower of Babel—the subject of a story in Genesis which indicates the widening gap which sin was creating between God and human society, as also among the various ancient peoples themselves

Tradition—the teachings of Jesus that were not written by the first Christians but passed on from the apostles through their successors. (Tradition was later written down, mainly in the official teachings of the Church)

Trinity—see Blessed Trinity

types—persons, or even things, in Scripture which can be recognized as foreshadowing later persons or things

typify—to foreshadow in some way

U

unleavened bread—bread made without leaven (yeast)—used by the Israelites to symbolize a fresh start at the beginning of the barley harvest. Eventually this feast was combined with the Passover celebration

V

versions of the Bible—different translations of the Bible, such as the following: Douay (Catholic); Jerusalem (Catholic); King James (Protestant); New American (Catholic); Revised Standard (Protestant, but also with a Catholic edition)

vestments—special clothes worn by those who lead a community at worship

Vicar of Christ—the person who takes Jesus' place on earth—the Pope

victim—whatever is offered to God in sacrifice

virgin—a person who has never experienced sexual intercourse

virtues—habits of doing good; habits that are holy (some examples are obedience, patience, charity...)

W

works of mercy—good deeds done for others out of love for God and people

worship—honoring and praising God; offering Him the gift of ourselves in the Mass and in other prayers; believing Him and doing what is right; worship as veneration (not adoration) is also given to the angels and saints

Y

Yahweh—the name under which God revealed Himself to the Israelites as the cause of everything that is

Z

Zeus—a Greek god, corresponding to the Roman Jupiter or Jove (the Lystrans mistook Barnabas for Zeus)

Zion—originally a Canaanite name for Jerusalem—still used for Jerusalem and sometimes for the Church

Index

Aaron 18, 26, 27, 28, 36
Abel 12
Abraham 12-15, 17, 29, 34, 39, 45, 59, 69
Absalom 39
Acts of the Apostles 111-129
Adam 9
Adonijah 40
adultery 39, 137
Advocate 96, 137
Ahab 42
Alexander the Great 47
Ammonites 37, 46
Amorites 32
Amos 42, 50
Andrew 61, 64, 70, 120
angel(s) 9, 106, 119, 120, 137
Anointed One 53
Anointing of the Sick 117, 137
Antioch (in Asia Minor) 121
Antioch (in Syria) 121, 122, 123, 125, 127
Antiochus IV 47
apocalyptic writing 51-52, 131-132, 137
apostles 4, 5, 70, 71, 73, 74, 90-102, 106-110, 111, 113-115, 116, 117, 118, 137
(see also **disciples** and individual first names)
Arabia 118
Aramaic language 124, 137
archaeologists 30, 32
Aristarchus 128
ark (of Noah) 12, 137
ark of the covenant 12, 26-27, 30, 33, 36, 39, 40, 44, 45, 137
ascension 93, 94, 115, 120, 121, 137
Asher 16
Assyrians 42, 50, 137
Baal 33, 41
Babel 12, 142
Babylon 44-46, 50, 51
Babylonian Exile 44-46, 50, 51, 123
Babylonians 43
Baptism 12, 32, 84, 108, 113, 116, 137

baptism of repentance 60-61
Barabbas 103, 113
Barnabas 119, 121-123
Bartholomew 70, 120
Baruch 52
beatitudes 62, 63, 137
Benjamin 16, 41
Bethany 78, 85-88, 90
Bethlehem 34-35, 37, 53, 57
Bible 4, 5-7, 8, 10, 132, 137
(see also **Old Testament, New Testament, Scriptures**)
bishop(s) 73, 74, 110, 116, 130, 137
Blessed Trinity 6, 58, 97, 99, 137
Boaz 35
Body of Christ
(see **Eucharist**)
body of Christ
(see **mystical body**)
bread of life 66
Caesar 104, 137
Cain 12
Caleb 27
calming of the sea 64
Cana 61
Canaan 13, 15, 17, 23, 27, 28, 29, 30ff., 137
Canaanites 32, 33, 41, 137
Capernaum 61-62
charity 137
(see also **love**)
cherubim 27, 137
chosen people 9, 15, 25, 26, 29, 33, 39ff., 112, 137
Christ 57, 59, 108, 114, 137
(see also **Jesus Christ**)
Christian(s) 56, 57, 62, 67, 68, 71, 78, 116, 121, 122, 123, 125, 129, 131, 132, 137
Christmas 57, 137
Chronicles 50
Church 5, 10, 12, 18, 57, 68, 69, 71, 72-73, 74, 88, 92, 110, 111, 112, 113, 115, 116, 117, 123, 126, 127, 129, 130, 132, 137
Colossians 129
commandments
(see **ten commandments**)

Communion 35, 94, 95, 138
(see also **Eucharist**)
communion of saints 99, 138
Confirmation 33, 116-117, 138
Consecration 66, 94, 138
conversion 42
Corinth 124, 126
Corinthians 126
Cornelius 119-120
Council of Jerusalem 122-123, 127
covenant 6, 13, 23, 24-25, 32-33, 59, 138
creation 8, 9, 138
crippled beggar 113-114
crucifixion 110, 130, 138
(see also **passion and death**)
Cyprus 121
Cyrus 46
Damascus 117, 118-119
Dan 16
Daniel 50-51, 83, 88, 132
David 35, 37-40, 52, 53, 57, 59, 69
deacon(s) 115, 116, 130, 138
death 88, 138
death and resurrection 111, 115, 121
(see also **passion and death** and **resurrection**)
Deborah 34, 69
Dedication 85
Deuteronomy 50, 53, 92
devil(s) 9, 10, 138
diaspora 123, 138
disciples 61, 62, 64, 67... 138
Easter 20, 106-108, 111, 138
Ecclesiastes 52
Ecclesiasticus 52
Egypt 13, 16ff., 27, 28, 30, 44, 47
Egyptians 17, 19-22, 26, 138
Eleazar (martyr) 48
Eleazar (son of Aaron) 28
Eli 36
Elijah 42, 72, 74
Elisha 42
Elizabeth 55, 56
Ephesians 129
Ephesus 125-126

Ephraim 32
epistles 138
(see also **letters**)
Esau 16
Essenes 81, 112, 138
Esther 50
eternal life 75
(see also **heaven**)
Eucharist 7, 52, 66, 68, 78, 84, 93-94, 98, 105, 113, 117, 138
Eucharistic Celebration
(see **Mass**)
Eve 9
evolution 9
Exile 138
(see also **Babylonian Exile**)
Exodus 22-29, 40, 61, 62, 74, 92, 93, 138
— book of 50
Ezekiel 44, 50, 98, 132
Ezra 47, 50
faith 70, 71, 83, 84, 86, 108, 113, 115, 116, 130, 138
Father 59, 63, 69, 79, 96, 97, 98, 101, 105, 107, 132, 138
fifth commandment 38, 39
first commandment 15
first parents 9
fortitude 70, 138
fourth commandment 34-35
future life 52
Gad 16
Galatians 125
Galileans 81
Galilee 64ff., 80, 109-110, 121, 138
Garden of Gethsemane 95, 96, 100-101
Genesis 8-16, 50, 107-108
Gentiles 47, 119, 120, 121, 122-123, 125, 126, 127, 128, 138
Gibeah 37
Gibeon 32
Gideon 34
God 5, 7, 8, 9, 10, 12-15, 16...116
(see also **Father, Yahweh, Jesus Christ, Holy Spirit**)

143

God's Name 18
golden bull 41
golden calf 26
Goliath 37
Good News 110, 112, 117, 118, 120, 121, 122, 123, 126
good Samaritan 50, 75-76, 78
Good Shepherd 83, 109
Gospels 6, 52, 57, 59, 62, 64, 66, 67, 68, 69, 78, 83, 90, 111, 117, 124
grace 9, 10, 11, 66, 70, 83, 84, 88, 98, 108, 110, 112, 124, 126, 138
Greek culture 47, 49, 52
Greek language 124, 138
Habakkuk 50
Haggai 46, 50
Hanukkah 48, 138
Hasmoneans 49
Hazor 32
heaven 4, 5, 52, 53, 66, 73, 88, 98, 138
Hebrew language 6, 138
Hebrew poetry 52
Hebrews 26, 138
 (see also **chosen people, Israelites, Jewish people**)
 —letter to 131
Hebron 39
hell 88, 138
Hermes 122, 138
Herod Antipas 85
Herod the Great 49
Hezekiah 43
high priest 47, 101, 138
historical books 50, 53, 54
Holy Orders 117, 119
Holy Spirit 5, 57, 61, 68, 72, 73, 83, 88, 96-97, 108, 111, 112, 113, 115, 116, 119, 120, 132, 139
hope 70, 139
Hosea 42, 50
humility 70, 139
Hyksos 16, 139
Immaculate Conception 70, 138
Incarnation 58, 59, 139
infallibility 73, 74, 139
inspiration 5, 139
Isaac 13-15, 17, 29
Isaiah 43, 50, 65, 69, 132
Israel 25, 33, 40, 41, 42, 45, 62, 98, 139
Israelites 17, 18ff., 139
Issachar 16
Jacob 16, 17, 29
James (apostle[s]) 70, 74, 100, 120
James (bishop of Jerusalem) 119, 122-123, 139
Jebusites 39
Jeremiah 43, 50, 69, 72, 98
Jericho 30, 32, 75, 86
Jeroboam 41
Jerusalem 32, 39, 43, 44, 45, 46, 47, 49, 52, 58, 60, 75, 78, 80-83, 86, 89, 90-105, 106, 107, 113, 115, 116, 119, 122-123, 125, 126, 127, 139
Jesus Christ 4-7, 10, 11, 20, 23, 25, 34, 52, 53, 54, 55-110, 111, 115, 117-118, 120, 122, 124, 125, 132
 —His name 57, 59, 139
Jewish people 47-49, 51, 112, 114, 115, 116, 117, 119, 120, 121, 122, 123, 124, 125, 126, 127, 139
Jewish religion 75
 (see also **chosen people, Judaism, Pharisees, Sadducees, Essenes**)
Jews
 (see **chosen people, Jewish people**, etc.)
Jezebel 42
Joanna 106
Job 52
Joel 50
John (apostle and/or Gospel of) 57, 67, 70, 71, 74, 83, 84, 90, 92, 95, 100, 104-105, 106, 109, 113-115, 116, 120, 122-123
John the Baptizer 55, 56, 60-61, 72, 85
Jonah 50
Jonathan (brother of Judas Maccabeus) 48, 49
Jonathan (son of Saul) 37, 38
Joppa 119, 120
Jordan River 29, 30, 61
Joseph (foster father of Jesus) 47, 57, 58, 59, 69
Joseph (son of Jacob) 16
Joseph of Arimathea 106
Joshua 27, 28, 30-33, 48, 50, 69

Josiah 43, 69
Judah (kingdom of) 41, 43-44, 45, 139
Judah (son of Jacob) 16
Judah (tribe of) 39, 47, 139
Judaism 47, 48, 49, 139
Judas (Iscariot) 70, 71, 92, 96, 120
Judas (Maccabeus) 48, 49, 69
Jude Thaddeus 70, 120
Judea 60, 88, 115, 117, 119, 121, 122, 139
Judges (book of) 50
judges 32, 33-35, 48, 139
Judith 50
Julius 128
justice 70, 139
Kadesh 27, 28
Kings 50
Lamentations 52
Last Supper 66, 90-98, 109, 117, 139
Lazarus of Bethany 85-89
Letter of James 117, 131
Letter(s) of John 131
Letter of Jude 131
Letter(s) of Paul 124, 125, 126, 129, 130
Letter(s) of Peter 131
Letter to the Hebrews 131
Levi 16, 32, 139
Levites 26, 32, 139
Leviticus 50
Light of the world 81
Liturgy of the Eucharist 94, 139
Liturgy of the Word 94, 139
Lord's Day 27
love (charity) 27, 70, 76-77, 79, 95, 139
Luke (evangelist and/or his Gospel) 57, 58, 67, 78, 111, 113, 121, 127, 128
Lystra 121-122, 123
Maccabees 48-49, 50, 51, 52, 88, 139
Malachi 50
Malta 128-129
man 9
Manasseh (king) 43
Manasseh (tribe) 32
manna 23, 30, 52, 66
Mark (evangelist and/or his Gospel) 57, 67
marriage 9, 117
Martha and Mary 78, 85-88
martyr(s) 48, 110, 130, 139
Mary, Blessed Virgin 55, 56, 57, 61, 62, 70, 74, 104-105, 106
Mary Magdalene 106-107
Mass 25, 27, 52, 66, 93-94, 113, 132, 139
Matrimony 117, 140
Mattathias 48
Matthew (apostle and/or Gospel of) 57, 62-63, 67, 70, 71-72, 120
Matthias 112, 120
mediator 70, 140
mercy seat 27
Mesopotamia 12
Messiah 53, 55, 56, 57, 61, 72, 74, 81, 84, 102, 103, 108, 115, 116, 118, 123, 127, 140
Micah 43, 50
Michal 37, 38
Midian 17
Midianites 34, 140
miracle(s) 42, 61-62, 64-66, 71, 112, 113, 116, 140
Miriam 22
Moab 29
Moabites 34-35, 140
Moses 17-29, 52-53, 62, 69, 74, 82-83
Mount Gilboa 38
Mount Hor 28
Mount Horeb 17, 23
Mount Nebo 29
Mount of Olives 86, 89, 90, 100
Mount Sinai 17, 23, 24, 26, 27, 29, 33, 62, 93, 112
multiplication of the loaves 64, 84
mystical body 99, 129, 140
Nahum 50
Naim 64
Naomi 34-35
Naphtali 16
Nathan 39, 40
Nazareth 55, 58
Nebuchadnezzar 43
Nehemiah 47, 50
neighbor 76-77
Nero 128
new covenant 54, 93, 140
New Testament 4, 6, 7, 10, 51, 55-132, 140

"new way" 115, 116, 121
Nicodemus 80
Ninevites 50
Noah 12
Numbers 50
Obadiah 50
Obed 35
obedience 70, 140
Old Testament 4, 5, 6, 7, 8-54, 57, 62, 66, 69, 74, 111, 114, 140
original sin 10, 70, 140
Our Father 63
Palestine 55, 56
 (see also **Canaan** and maps throughout the text)
parable(s) 50, 140
Paraclete 96, 140
 (see also **Holy Spirit**)
"parousia" 124
paschal lamb 19, 20, 52, 89, 90, 92, 140
passion and death 66, 73, 74, 88-89, 93, 94, 95, 100-105, 109, 114, 117
Passover 20, 30, 52, 58, 89, 90-93, 103, 140
patriarchs 16, 140
Paul (Saul) 111, 115, 117-119, 120, 121-130, 131
Penance 78, 108, 110, 117, 140
Pentecost 111-112, 120, 140
people of God 6, 112, 123
 (see also **chosen people and Church**)
Perea 60, 85, 140
persecution 47, 48, 51-52, 115, 116, 117, 122, 124, 130, 131, 132, 140
Persians 46, 47, 140
Peter 57, 61, 62, 70, 71-74, 90, 91, 92, 95, 100, 101-102, 106, 109-110, 111, 112, 113-115, 116, 119-120, 122-123, 130, 131
pharaoh 16, 17, 18, 19, 21, 43, 140
Pharisees 81, 82, 83, 86, 88, 89, 92, 103, 112, 115, 140
Philemon 129
Philip (apostle) 64, 70, 96, 120
Philip (deacon) 116
Philippi 123, 125
Philippians 125
Philistines 32, 34, 36, 37, 38, 39, 140
Phoenicia 121, 140
pilgrims 89, 90, 100, 140
Pilate 102-104
pillar of cloud 21, 22
plague(s) 19, 140
Pope 73, 74, 110, 130, 140
prayer 62, 70, 78-79, 141
 (see also **Mass, sacrifice**)
presbyters 122, 141
priests (Christian) 93, 95, 108, 122, 130, 141
priests (Hebrew) 26, 28, 30, 37, 88, 141
Profession of Faith 94
prophet(s) 36, 39, 40, 41, 42, 43, 44, 45, 46, 50-52, 53-54, 59, 60, 61, 72, 74, 82...141
Proverbs 52
providence 6, 17, 23, 141
prudence 70, 141
Psalms 52, 53, 92, 93, 141
Ptolemies 47, 141
purgatory 88, 98, 141
Qoheleth 52
Qumran 55, 81, 141
Red Sea 25
 (see also **Sea of Reeds**)
religion 13, 141
repentance 113, 116, 141
resurrection of Jesus 4, 5, 6, 73, 86, 93, 94, 106-108, 109, 110, 114, 141
 (see also **death and resurrection**)
resurrection of the dead 52, 88, 141
Reuben 16
Revelation 131-132
revelation 5, 10, 52, 132, 141
Romans 81, 102-104, 126, 128, 130
Rome 65, 129, 130
Ruth 34-35, 50, 69
Sabbath 23, 27, 81, 82, 141
sacraments 66, 83-84, 116-117, 120, 132, 141
sacrifice 93, 94, 141
Sadducees 81, 92, 112, 114, 141
saint(s) 69, 70, 141
salvation 5, 10, 11, 57, 117, 126, 141

salvation history 10, 11, 17, 50, 111, 115, 120, 132, 141
Samaria 115, 116, 121, 141
Samaritans 42, 46, 76, 116, 141
Samson 33
Samuel 36-37
 —books of 50, 53
Sarah 13
Saul (apostle)
 (see **Paul**)
Saul (king) 37, 38, 39
Savior 26, 52-53, 109, 117, 123, 141
 (see also **Jesus Christ**)
Scripture(s) 4, 5, 47, 88, 94, 117, 120, 132, 141
 (see also **Old Testament** and **New Testament**)
Sea of Galilee 64, 71, 109
Sea of Reeds 21, 30, 61, 141
second commandment 18
"Second Isaiah" 45, 50, 113
Seleucids 47, 48, 141
Septuagint 47
sermon on the mount 62-63, 141
"Servant of Yahweh" 113
seventh commandment 42
Shechem 32
Shiloh 33, 36
sickness 117
Silas 123
Simeon 16
Simon (apostle) 70, 120
Simon (brother of Judas Maccabeus) 48, 49
Simon Peter
 (see **Peter**)
sin(s) 9, 10, 11, 12, 60, 81, 88, 108, 113, 117, 142
Sirach 52
sixth commandment 34, 39
social justice 42, 76-77
Solomon 40-41
"Son of David" 55, 56
Son of God 85, 86
"Son of Man" 83
Song of Songs 52
soul 9, 142
Stephen 115, 116
suffering servant 53
Sunday 27
Susanna 106
synagogue 119
tabernacle 26, 142
Tarsus 119
temperance 70, 142
temple 39, 40, 44, 45, 46, 47, 48, 49, 74, 85, 112-113, 115, 128, 142
ten commandments 24, 25, 26, 27, 47, 62, 70, 76, 123, 125
Thaddeus
 (see **Jude Thaddeus**)
Thessalonians 124
Thessalonica 123, 124
third commandment 27
Thomas 70, 86, 96, 108, 120
Timothy 123, 130
Titus 130
Tobit 50
Tradition 5, 88, 117, 120, 132, 142
transfiguration 74
translations 124
truth 83
twelve tribes 32
type(s) 52-53, 54, 142
Vatican II 77
Vicar of Christ 73, 142
virtues 70, 142
vine and branches 98-99
walking on the water 71
way, truth and life 96
Wisdom 52, 53, 88
wisdom books 52, 53, 54
witnessing 62
woman 9
Word of God 66, 68
 (see also **Bible, Scriptures, Old Testament, New Testament**)
works of mercy 70, 77, 79, 142
Yahweh 18, 20, 22, 23, 24, 25, 26, 28, 30, 33, 36...81, 96, 108, 123, 142
Zadok 40
Zealots 81
Zebulun 16
Zechariah (father of John the Baptizer) 55
Zechariah (prophet and/or his writings 46, 50, 89, 132
Zephaniah 50
Zerubbabel 46
Zeus 47, 122, 142